Facing Apocalypse

Facing Apocalypse

Climate, Democracy,
and Other Last Chances

CATHERINE KELLER

ORBIS BOOKS
Maryknoll, New York 10545

Founded in 1970, Orbis Books endeavors to publish works that enlighten the mind, nourish the spirit, and challenge the conscience. The publishing arm of the Maryknoll Fathers and Brothers, Orbis seeks to explore the global dimensions of the Christian faith and mission, to invite dialogue with diverse cultures and religious traditions, and to serve the cause of reconciliation and peace. The books published reflect the views of their authors and do not represent the official position of the Maryknoll Society. To learn more about Orbis Books, please visit our website at www.orbisbooks.com.

Thanks to April Pederson for permission to reprint the cartoon on p. 41.
Excerpts from *Appalachian Elegy* © 2012 by Gloria Jean Watkins (bell hooks), published by the University Press of Kentucky, used with permission.
"Hallelujah" by Leonard Cohen, collected in STRANGER MUSIC: Selected Poems and Songs. Copyright © 1993 by Leonard Cohen and Leonard Cohen Stranger Music, Inc., used by permission of The Wylie Agency LLC.

Manufactured in the United States of America

Library of Congress Cataloging-in-Publication Data
Names: Keller, Catherine, author.
Title: Facing apocalypse : climate, democracy, and other last chances / Catherine Keller.
Description: Maryknoll, NY : Orbis Books, [2021] | Includes bibliographical references and index. | Summary: "The biblical Apocalypse of John offers a lens for considering the apocalyptic challenges of our time"— Provided by publisher.
Identifiers: LCCN 2020043739 (print) | LCCN 2020043740 (ebook) | ISBN 9781626984134 (print) | ISBN 9781608338771 (ebook)
Subjects: LCSH: Bible. Revelation—Criticism, interpretation, etc.
Classification: LCC BS2825.52 .K45 2021 (print) | LCC BS2825.52 (ebook) | DDC 228/.06—dc23
LC record available at https://lccn.loc.gov/2020043739
LC ebook record available at https://lccn.loc.gov/2020043740

Contents

PreScroll

Hamlet: *What news?*
Rosencrantz: *None, my lord, but that the world's grown honest.*
Hamlet: *Then is doomsday near.*

—*William Shakespeare*

It isn't as if we don't know better. It isn't as though we can't do better. Millennia ago, even after the growth of global empires, there were communities practicing an ethos of care for each other, for strangers, for aliens, for the whole creation. There were teachers on record denouncing systems of oppression, announcing the renewal of the earth. So are there now. Not all of us, maybe not most of us, live out of sync with our biology, which, according to recent science, favors cooperation over competition. Why the endless triumph of greed and power? One of those ancient teachers denounced the global economics and politics of his time in language that sounds eerily relevant to ours. He wrote a long scroll of a letter warning that the news would get worse, much worse, before it gets—better? Why are we still acting out the dark dreams of John's *Apocalypse*?

That book, also known as *Revelation*, the final text of the Christian Bible, takes the form of a letter written to several young communities of Asia Minor, part of the Roman Empire at the end of the first century. The author John (often confused with the author of the Gospel of John) wrote from exile, voluntary or otherwise, on the Greek island of Patmos, off the west coast of Asia. He penned his scroll in a carefully coded language profoundly critical of the empire that had colonized what for him counted as the known world. Many theologians from the beginning, later including Luther, expressed ambivalence about this letter's authoritative status. Nonetheless, with its barely veiled politics, its metaphoric munificence, and its dramatic clues to collective trauma and hope, the Apocalypse retained, indeed retains, its climactic position within the Christian canon.

That climax has read out differently, in religious or in secular terms, from one age to the next. Now our age is threatening its own distinctively "apocalyptic" climax: climate havoc. Yet for decades the rhetoric of The End of the World could be left largely to fundamentalist or sci-fi fantasy. Except for some last-century nuclear alarms, any Apocalypses Now not marked "fiction" could be dismissed as hysterical. But in our present tense, altogether credible sources declare "the Insect Armageddon," "the Uninhabitable Earth," "Climate Doom"—and of course the "Anthropocene Apocalypse." Visiting friends out west a year ago, I was startled by the headline of a local newspaper: "Earth's future is being written in rapidly melting Greenland ice." The article quotes a respected air and ocean scientist inferring from that meltdown "the end of the planet."[1] Though lacking Hamlet's tragic irony, such ecological announcements seem now all too tragically honest—scientifically, publicly. But for several decades a broad public was able to snigger at such "apocalyptic" warnings.

The snigger however is twisting into a frown. As it happened—in a past millennium—it was fear of nuclear holocaust that first

---

1. "He is referring to geography more than the future," the newspaper reassures us. See Seth Borenstein, "Earth's Future Is Being Written in Fast-Melting Greenland," *The Associated Press* (August 20, 2019).

pushed me into a serious engagement with the Christian End-of-the-World tradition. My suspicion was *not* that the *Book of Revelation*, a.k.a. *Apocalypse of John*, was finally going to be proven right. No, I was realizing that the long Western imagination of The End was serving as a self-fulfilling prophecy: its blood-soaked narrative had worked for centuries to justify righteous waves of Christian and then secular violence. And both together. So we had through the 1980s a president who was buddy-buddy with the author of *The Late Great Planet Earth*. These guys smugly concurred that thermonuclear exchange would bring on the Endtimes in their lifetimes. One of them had a finger on the nuclear button. Since it seemed that in the United States liberal/progressive theologians were ignoring the apocalypse and its effects, I got to work.

Fortunately by the time *Apocalypse Now and Then: A Feminist Approach to the End of the World* was done, the nuclear threat had dissipated. And while researching I had realized that I couldn't simply write off the last book of the Bible—despite its bitter determinism, its misogynist, good/evil dualism, its forecasts of violent mass death. There was something more to its radical vision. Turns out that all the Western egalitarian or revolutionary movements, the fights for democracy, socialism, women's rights, emancipation of slaves, right on through Martin Luther King's "dream," tapped apocalyptic metaphors of great tribulation and transformation. In their struggle for a "new heaven and earth," for a just and sustainable life for all, they draw from the ancient Jewish prophetic tradition of the "new creation." Including, very prominently, John's Apocalypse and its New Jerusalem.

Yet the dangerous hope for a final, one-off destruction and salvation persists—largely but not exclusively on the right. It feeds the presumption that history and nature move down linear tracks to the Last Stop. Because it exercises great cultural force, that presumption of The End needs to be repeatedly deconstructed.

And the deconstruction requires the *theological* alternatives on offer from fresh visions of the world. Those evolving narratives, mindful of sex, race, class, ecology, etc.—oh that edgy etc.—let me become and remain a theologian. They include theologies of deep pluralism, engaged in interreligious interchange and multiple secular practices. Denouncing injustice and announcing ecosocial healing, these legacies of prophetic discourse persist. As does their spirited timeliness. Whatever ends, of whatever times, we must confront.

Something however has changed, and, eerily, in this young millennium. The End can no longer be mocked as simple delusion, as religious dope-hope, or as the by-product of some analogous, secular use-it-all-up progress. The "now and then" of my 1996 title is a bit off. We are living through a singularity. While much social, political, and ecological degradation can still be stopped, something irreversible has after all kicked in. Something measurable in a creepy couple of degrees of global warming. A process with effects beyond measure. Is it a viable candidate for The End of the World? No. But possibly of the human world. Then Covid-19 galloped in—not dooming our species but exposing the interlinked precarity of U.S. democracy, global economics, and planetary health. The coronavirus was not caused by global warming, but the fever of its victims and the fever of the planet seem together to pose a dire collective warning. That would be the biblical sense of *apokalypsis*, "revelation." Humans have come out of all balance with each other and with the nonhuman. Has the pandemic pause helped us *face* this apocalypse? To heed its warning somewhere between the overstated and the unspeakable?

In the early nineteenth century, Søren Kierkegaard, that most ironic of theologians, had no more of a concept of climate change than did Shakespeare. Still, his parable, set on a different stage, rings prophetic: "It happened that a fire broke out backstage in a theater. The clown came out to inform the public. They thought it was a jest and applauded. He repeated his warning. They shouted even louder. So I think the world will come to an end amidst the general applause from all the wits who believe that it is a joke."[2] Environmentalists have often felt like that clown.

As the smoke bellows into the theater of present history, the laughter is fading. The heat is rising. The political forces that might rein in an economy driven by carbon emissions, that might foster green new deals and needed strategies for extracting excess carbon from the atmosphere, have instead deferred or downright denied responsibility for climate change. (The science denialism runs deep and deadly, as pandemically demonstrated in a president's disregard of epidemiological advice.) In the meantime the nobler social forces must contend with the lurching systemic immensity of racial, social, economic injustice. To focus on the nonhuman environment can seem *in*human. Yet to sideline ecology means, now, to leave those human populations who contribute the least to global warming to suffer its worst effects.

Should we now press the alarm button—Greta Thunberg's "time to panic"—in hopes of cutting through the white noise of climate denialism? Or, to the contrary, should we keep a more positive tone in order to avoid doomsday nihilism?[3] Or neither? Or both? With each new round of "unprecedented" fire or flood, melting or mass migration, we will stretch for language and find the apocalypse—right there where we hope to avoid it. Conscious

---

2. Søren Kierkegaard, *Either/Or*, vol. 1, trans. David F. Swenson and Lillian Marvin Swenson (Princeton, NJ: Princeton University Press, 1971), 30.

3. Michael Shellenberger, *Apocalypse Never: Why Environmental Alarmism Hurts Us All* (New York: Harper, 2020).

or subliminal, ironic or menacing, the rhetoric of apocalypse will be amping up for the "foreseeable future." Whatever we can and cannot foresee about our planetary future, echoes of the ancient Apocalypse will henceforth reverberate not just across wide varieties of religion but in responsible forms of secular discourse. For this reason I hope that you—you of *whatever* or of *no* religious persuasion—will stay with the present meditation.

If apocalypticism cannot be erased, it must be *minded*: used *mindfully*, that is not for mindless fright or melodrama, not for supernatural or sci-fi flight. To attend to its actual meaning becomes key to redirecting its present energies. And make no mistake: the energies conducted by the antique figuration of the Apocalypse remain relentless, contradictory, effectual. For good and for ill. The feedback loop between archaic prophecy and future history swirls through the present. The text refuses to stop and become simply literal, fixed in one particular final realization.

Despite garish religious outbreaks, the metaphors of apocalypse circulate mostly below the surface. So surfacing its effects, making and keeping them conscious, will be necessary to the work of ecological and social response for—that foreseeable future. Mindfulness of the apocalypse can keep us from acting it out in private despair or collective inevitability, playing it out subliminally in our economic habits, democratic disarray, and ecological suicide. We have a chance of pausing the self-fulfilling prophecy of doom. And that interruption, prolonged, might prove truer to the original Apocalypse than mere annihilation.

The eery synchronicity of the ancient imaginary with contemporary history does sometimes give one pause. As it has throughout history. For example, the pale green horse of John's vision carries the fourth horseman of the Apocalypse, releasing the inhuman force of "pestilence." Plagues have frequently and with terrifying effect galloped across the world. In John's vision the

green horse is soon followed—after a dramatic pause in heaven—
by the opening of the seventh seal, which as we will see in the
present book's second chapter, warns of the destruction of forests,
oceans, and fresh waters. To *mind* such metaphors is to recognize
that John is *not predicting future facts*. But he may be *revealing
fatal patterns*. We read the images for meditation and for confrontation. Might facing the Apocalypse in its ancient intensity help us
face apocalypse in our own time? Such "facing" would not mean
mere recognition, submission, acquiescence. It means to confront
the forces of destruction: to crack open, to disclose, a space where
late chances, last chances, remain nonetheless real chances.

The metaphor of apocalypse—really, metaphor is too weak a
notion, why not call it *metaforce*—has been playing itself out for
a couple of millennia. It has affected religious as well as political,
reactionary as well as revolutionary movements. It presents overtly
and covertly. It refracts in a hallucinatory multiplicity of modes.
Sometimes aggressively preached, often unconsciously transmitted, its forcefield is not immutable or predetermined. Neither is
it fading. Given the historical power and the future inevitability
of its metaforce, I am gambling that a curation of some of its past
stories in their contexts, ancient and recent, will help alter current
consciousness.

John's Apocalypse remains always the text of an ancient context.
The first-century BCE text of Revelation was written with no concept of a "Bible," let alone of its own coming canonization within
one. Its visions were apparently recorded for inclusion in a letter to
be read aloud in different early Christian communities scattered
throughout the Roman Empire. John addresses each specifically,
in praise and critique. The text's dramatic mode of anti-imperial
witness belongs to the movement of Jewish apocalypticism, which

was not some marginal bit of extremism but a late metamorphosis of Hebrew prophecy. Apocalypticism, as a leading German biblical scholar put it, "was the mother of all Christian theology."[4]

The reverb between the ancient letter's context and our own pervades the present text—a work not of biblical history but of meditation on the present. We do not read the old scroll for its own sake. Rather, we let its old imaginary, directed at its own context, release surprising relevancies for ours. And we read them not because the ancient visions *predict* present realities. Forgive me, this needed repetition: *prophecy* is not *prediction*. If in some surreal sense their author does prophesy it is not because he was seeing the future. Only what already exists can be seen. And the future is what does not yet exist. But deep patterns do exist in the present. And they may long persist. A prophet reads a potent pattern of human civilization—a pattern that may still, in some strange and tragic ways, replicate itself today. Or so we may meaningfully read it.

With or without religious beliefs, therefore, with or without curiosity about John's Apocalypse, you are invited into this reading of a reading. Of something like a dream state in urgent need of interpretation, one with a darkly collective space and time. You may find that engaging some of its eerily animated figures will help you face your own, *our* own, nightmares—of, for instance, a climate-forced collapse of civilization within not many years, escalating mass migration and starvation, white supremacism, degrees of fascism, elite escapes, population decimation, and possibly worse. . . .

Prophecy then or now *dreamreads* a collective context. Within the patterns of what has already become, it attends to what might

<hr>

4. Ernst Käsemann, "The Beginnings of Christian Theology," in *New Testament Questions of Today*, trans. W. J. Montague (London: SCM, 1969), 102.

yet be. Possibilities, chances, good and ill. Unrealized possibility has a dreamlike quality—it shadows the real. The Apocalypse as text is itself full of dreamreadings. Reading them, we in turn will dreamread the apocalypse. Crowded, clouded, with prophetic metaphors, the ancient text serves here as a pre-text of our current context. As we read a few scraps of the old scroll we may find—in defiance of the doomsday stereotype—that its critical message carries not just high levels of inevitable catastrophe but far better possibilities.

Facing Apocalypse suggests first of all that there will be in our time no *honest* escape from the notion of apocalypse, and therefore from the question of its meaning. For whatever happens socially, politically, pandemically, and economically, global warming is sure to keep the metaforce charged. Not (she repeats) because predictions of an ancient text are finally "coming true." Nor because the Bible or any of its books is "true at all times in all places for all people." Truth is not something fixed in advance. Truth does not banish uncertainty. Truth invites questioning. It does not transcend its context of tangled relations, but it may transform their meaning. If truth has something to do with honesty. With facing.

Holding our collective twenty-first-century context in relation to the ancient one, the present book is to be read as a way of ecopolitical practice. Like much contemplative practice, it aims through meditation, imagination, and conversation at actualization. Of what is—actually—possible.

Since it will be henceforth impossible to avoid the charged language of apocalypse—to ignore it as cliché or archaicism, to dismiss it for its vengeful and patriarchal violence—why not take some time to understand it? Might it help us to read this "time" that we are running out of? Might we be helped to give ourselves, to give each other, time? Each other: others not merely of human-kind—but mineral, vegetable, animal kinds? All the kinds with which we form our world? For a "world" exists as the timely context of its inhabitants. Worlds, in that sense, have ended over and over—in conquest and in enslavement, in human genocide, in nonhuman extinctions, but also in radical change.

If something else is happening now, it is what this dreamreading practice will keep surfacing: the one earth of all those diverse "worlds" is in recoil. Its capacity to hold us, to host us, through innumerable endings, new beginnings, emergencies, emergences, to give our species always another opportunity to get it right—this, for so long, we could presume. Humans could commit all manner of atrocities in the name of their own world, land, folk, *Volk*. But we could at least take for granted the humanly habitable planet. That grant seems to be running out. Impending climate disaster has brought us—no, not to the Endtimes—but to a time of manifold last chances. So apocalyptic urgency pulses in a new way through the spectrum of human struggles: thus one Black Lives Matter group marched under the banner "Last Chance for Change."[5]

Hamlet's irony doubles back upon us. Will the world grow honest enough to change course—only when it is too late? Will what wakes us up be what takes us out?

Nonetheless, and no matter what doomsdays we face: the Greek term used in the New Testament, *apokalypsis,* does not signify "the end of the world." Not time's up, lights out. Close down the creation. On the contrary, it means not to close but to *dis/close.* To *open* what is otherwise shut. Originally the word signified the sexually charged moment of an ancient bride's unveiling. That erotic metaforce infuses John's feminized and final sign, the joy-

---

5. Chris Libonati, "Last Chance for Change Marchers Attract a Sudden Following; Where Will It Lead?" *Syracuse* (June 7, 2020).

ous utopia of "New Jerusalem." To uncover apocalypse—now and then—is to open multiple registers of affect. Registers traumatic and mournful, furious, festive, hopeful. And ironic.

We will read the phantasmagoric imagery of the Apocalypse like a vast dream. We may even observe global nightmare twist toward weirdly attractive possibility. I'm not claiming that any dreamreading of a shadowy book of ancient visions will magically heal our society's collective sickness, our species' environ-*mental* illness. Amidst its tensions and its traumas, its past futures and failed hopes, the old scroll may finally dissolve into its archaic context. But in the process its very antiquity can help us scroll down deeper into a shared present tense, the tense present of our planetary public.

Recapocalypse

The present text unfolds in the shape of seven chapters, each of which faces a particular figure of the Apocalypse. It follows the sequence of the old scroll, not exhaustively, not narrating the text for its own sake, but inasmuch as a synchronistic story emerges for our present sakes. There follows below a brief recapitulation of the narrative of the Book of Revelation itself, as I do not presume the reader's familiarity with the biblical text. The twenty-two chapters of Revelation are here cloud-clumped into the seven figurations of my book. But this outline recaps the Apocalypse as background—not as outline—of the present dreamreading. Readers might check it anytime they want more clarity about the biblical narrative. Of course they are more than welcome to check out the original—specific chapters and verses are consistently designated.[1]

This text from the first century CE was written as a letter addressed to seven emergent congregations. As they were all subjects of Rome, John of Patmos encrypts his critique of the Empire in a dense ancient symbolism. In the tradition of such Hebrew prophets as Isaiah, Amos, Daniel, and Ezekiel, John delivers the message as the content of multiple visions. That outpouring of

---

1. All biblical quotations come from the New Revised Standard Version (National Council of the Churches of Christ, 1989), unless otherwise noted with "K," in which case they are from Craig R. Koester, *Revelation: A New Translation with Introduction and Commentary,* Anchor Bible (New Haven: Yale University Press, 2014).

dream-like images gets pressed by John into a narrative extend-
ing through his twenty-two chapters. For purposes of convenient
reference, I here outline the sequence of visions, divided into the
seven signs forming the chapters of *Facing Apocalypse*.

1. Announcing himself as "the Alpha and the Omega," the one
   "coming with the clouds" appears, looking "like a human
   being" (1:7–9). And after John gets out his specific greetings
   and admonitions to the communities of the way, the visions
   flow. The "throne of God" appears, surrounded by throned
   elders, and also by "four living creatures" (4:1–11). Then a scroll
   with seven seals presents, which only "the Lion of the tribe of
   Judah" can open; but instead the Lamb (looking slaughtered)
   turns up to do the honors. Upon the opening of each of the first
   four seals, a differently colored horse appears, bearing diverse
   violence, injustice, and plagues. The fury of worldwide devastation continues—while 144,000 servants of God are "sealed"
   protectively—until there comes, before the opening of the seventh seal, a "silence in heaven" (chaps. 6–8).

2. Now seven angels with trumpets step up, and another sequence
   of seven plays out as each blows. The first trumpet reveals fire
   burning "one-third of the trees," the next the death of a third
   of sea life, then the poisoning of fresh waters, then more horror of quake, smoke, and fiery destruction to sky and earth
   (chaps. 8, 9). Another pause, while John is told to take and eat a
   little scroll, sweet in his mouth but bitter to his stomach—and
   prophesy some more (chap. 10). The last blast: "God's wrath"
   promises to reward the faithful, "the small and the great, and
   to destroy those who destroy the earth" (11:16).

3. Now the "great sign" materializes: "a woman clothed with the
   sun, with the moon under her feet and a wreath of twelve stars
   on her head," pregnant, crying out "in the agony of giving birth"

(12:1ff.). A fiery, red, seven-headed dragon appears, knocks down "a third of the stars" and lands before the woman, ready to devour the infant as it emerges. But the child is "snatched away" to heaven, and the woman flees into the wilderness. The furious dragon (or "devil") then loses a battle in heaven, and thrown down to earth pursues the woman. She is rescued by the Earth. So he goes after "the rest of her offspring" (followers of the Law and of Jesus; 12:17).

4. Now the dragon is joined by a seven-headed beast from the sea, and a two-horned beast from the earth, who forces all humankind to worship an idol of the first beast and bear its mark: "666" (13:18). Now in a bitter vintage the earth is reaped, thrown like grapes into "the great winepress of the wrath of God," overflowing as blood. Then the seven bowls of rage are poured onto the planet, with ecologically deadening effect, battle of Armageddon, and a fury of storms (chaps. 15, 16).

5. That seven-bowl angel takes John to see "the judgment of the great whore ... with whom the kings of the earth have committed fornication, and with the wine of whose fornication the inhabitants of the earth have become drunk" (17:1–3). This new "Babylon the Great" rides the red seven-headed beast— who with the kings suddenly turns on her, strips and devours her (17:16). The rulers lament; and the sea and land merchants of global trade "weep and mourn for her, since no one buys their cargo anymore, cargo of gold, silver, jewels [etc., etc.]— and human lives" (18:11–13).

6. There is great celebration at New Babylon's fall, followed by the "marriage supper of the Lamb." But there follows the judgment of the beasts and the dragon, and amidst a final fury of battle, another dinner: the punishing "great Supper of God" (chap. 19). A judgment of all, the thousand-year rule of the martyrs, a last planetary battle, a final fiery verdict, and "the

second death" for all humans whose names fail to show up in the book of life. . . .

7. And finally: John "saw a new heaven and a new earth," beyond suffering and death. God comes down to dwell with humanity in the New Jerusalem—who is the Lamb's marriage partner, the sparkling post-imperial city (chap. 21). The River of Life runs through the city, with water as a gift for all who thirst, and a multiple Tree of Life bearing fruit for "the healing of the nations." John adds his own curses to the blessings. The book ends with the grace of a renewed blessing and the promise of the coming of the Alpha–Omega (chap. 22).

1

O Clouds Unfold
Dreamreading the Apocalypse

Look! He is coming with the clouds.
                                        —Revelation 1:7

There's a cloud floating in, disarmingly fluffy. It curls sun-shine into glowing shadows. As you stare, the soft mass shifts majestically. It seems to be sweeping in; you can't tell how fast. Keep watching. The cloud morphs into cumulus curls, into white, wooly hair upon a darkness smooth as skin. Like a tongue, like a sword, rays pierce the cloud. It turns into one big wooly lamb. As the four-legged cloud swells in poignant dignity, the setting sun bleeds red across its fur.

That is one way to paraphrase the first three appearances of the Messiah in the biblical Apocalypse.

Or then again, if you are interested, I will cite chapter and verse. But why would you be? You may occasionally use the term "apocalypse" to voice your rising fear for the world, but you are just using a common metaphor for macro-catastrophe. You are probably not alluding to the Book of Revelation. And whatever you think about the Bible, odds are (since you have gotten this far) you are no *Left Behind* fan, eager to be raptured up to those clouds to meet your Lord.[1] We just don't have another word with quite the cataclysmic oomph of *apocalypse*. It captures the drama of unprecedented threats to human civilization and to planetary health. And anyway, to say "this is an apocalyptic moment" is not necessarily to trumpet The End of the World.

No, not necessarily. An alarm is not a requiem. But chances may be looking lousy for the persistence of the world-as-we-know-it. And just what do we "know," anyway—even if we accept, for instance, the climate science? Those who don't can drift with the prevailing denialism. But many of those who *get* the science now sink into a savvy nihilism. They see hope as delusional, and so surrender to the spiral of our species' self-destruction. I'm imagining, however, that *you* do not rule out the possibility of a livable planetary future—one even including humans. The *possibility*: if, against considerable odds, some collective upsurge of urgency prevails. Before our planetary emergency goes total.

I'm with you.

To help each other out of the sleepily creeping patterns of species suicide, without just waking into despair: this motivates a "dreamreading" of our apocalypse. And with it, of the Apocalypse. Let the lower case signify the perilous present context, and the upper, the two-millennia-old text. But why put our present tense in touch with the strange surrealism of the ancient Apocalypse? Because it is already at work in current history; and more importantly, because our reading of the connection will help to awaken a collective *possibility*. Such possibility does not drift on the surface of day-to-day normalcy. Nor do our chances offer themselves as commodity choices. They appear increasingly as *last* chances. Not "Endtimes" but narrowing options.

---

1. *Left Behind*, the series of sixteen bestselling novels by Tim LaHaye and Jerry B. Jenkins, rendered so far as four films, dramatizes the dispensationalist evangelical reading of the apocalyptic Endtimes.

The ancient script has somehow not exhausted itself, even after century upon century of false Endtime predictions. As a literary critic once put it, "Apocalypse can be disconfirmed without being discredited. This is part of its extraordinary resilience."[2] Indeed, beneath the hyper-familiar clichés—warrior Christ, Last Judgment, pearly gates—the original Apocalypse surprises. It reads more like a waking dream than a plan for history. We will observe how its phantasmagoric metaphors of unresolved trauma and unrealized healing open into tensions of present history: our present. If in the irony of a vast anachronism we let our own grief, concern, and curiosity into our reading, the process may prove darkly disclosive.

In recognizing an ancient history as somehow still our own, its darkness yields more than nightmare. A cloud of roiling possibility seems to reveal itself. It seems barely distinct from impossibility. It guarantees no happy ending. It may, however, enhance the uncertain chance of better outcomes. It is for the sake of that chance that we might practice, in and beyond this reading, an *apocalyptic mindfulness*. Such darkly glowing possibility might justify, even invite, reconsideration of this long letter of John of Patmos, this Apocalypse, in the archaisms and in the futures of its dizzying metaphors.

We will spiral between the text of the Apocalypse and our own context, with its apocalyptic charge. The ancient text reads the crisis of its own historical context. It does not know or predict ours. But it discerns certain patterns in its own world deep enough to persist, dangerously, and perhaps disclosively, into our own. To *mind* those patterns without literalizing them means to dreamread collective crisis now, by way of the metaphors—the metaforce—of the Apocalypse then.

---

2. Frank Kermode, *The Sense of an Ending: Studies in the Theory of Fiction* (New York: Oxford University Press, 2000), 8.

1. Armageddonesque

The narrative metaforce of the Apocalypse fires up effects secular as well as religious, fictional as well as historical. Consider for instance Kim Stanley Robinson's novel *New York 2140,* an important development of the literary genre of climate fiction (cli-fi, as distinct from sci-fi). A twenty-second-century character referred to as "that citizen" comments sardonically on the two "Pulses" of catastrophic coastal flooding that the planet had undergone at the end of the twenty-first century:

> All that happened very quickly, in the very last years of the twenty-first century. Apocalyptic, Armageddonesque, pick your adjective of choice. Anthropogenic could be one. Extinctional another. Anthropogenic mass extinction event, the term often used. End of an era. Geologically speaking, it might rather be the end of an age, period, epoch, or aeon, but that can't be decoded until it has run its full course, so the common phrase "end of an era" is acceptable for the next billion or so years, after which we can revise the name appropriately.[3]

The year 2140 sounds reassuringly distant. As do the aeonic billion years. In the meantime we may find ourselves, along with that ironic citizen, reaching for adjectives of the unbearable. "Apocalyptic" not surprisingly heads the list. Global warming, with its few ruinous degrees of average annual temperature, is now well on its way to sealing the future (nonfictionally speaking) with doom: in floods, droughts, and fires, in extinctions of endless fellow species, in systemic human-on-human violence amplified by white supremacism, mounting climate migrations, and class injustice. As to the economic causes of the environmental catastrophes, that citi-

---

3. Kim Stanley Robinson, *New York 2140* (London: Orbit, 2017), 144.

zen notes: "Never had so much been done to so many by so few!"
He means not the few degrees but the 1 percent, who relentlessly
funded and forced climate change denial for the sake of carbon-
driven hyper-profits.

None of Robinson's cast of characters is religious, though several are manifestly ethical. Yet this fictional deployment of "apocalyptic" turns out to be more faithful to historic reality—and with
it also to the original meaning of the metaphor—than much religious apocalypticism. The novel's social ecology never becomes
theology. Without giving away the ending, I can say that its apocalypse does not mean mere shut-down, human extinction, or even
hopeless ecosocial degradation. Whatever ends in *New York 2140*,
it is not "the world." Not even necessarily civilization, *civis*—"city."
Between catastrophic shifts, Robinson's protagonists develop as
lively urban improvisers rather than retro-paleo-survivalists.

Apokalypsis, the Greek word for "revelation," means literally
the "removal of the veil." It means not closure but *dis-closure*—that
is, opening. A chance to open our eyes? John's ancient narrative
imagines a future of late chances, last chances. Now the narratives
of cli-fi, and indeed of cli-sci, unveil entrenched civilizational patterns with dire interhuman, interspecies, planetary consequences.
Increasingly, mainstream media evince this apocalyptic honesty.
Amidst pandemic resurgence, antiracist protest, political panic,
and climate sidelining, *Time* magazine headlined, "One Last
Chance: The Defining Year for the Planet." Justin Worland writes
that "In the future, we may look back at 2020 as the year we
decided to keep driving off the climate cliff—or to take the
last exit."[4] In retrospect, each following year may prove no less
defining. But the *apokalypsis* of last chances only gains in reveal-

---

4. Justin Worland, "2020 Is Our Last, Best Chance to Save the
Planet," *Time* (July 9, 2020).

ing relevance. Ripping off the veil of normalcy offers the chance, the choice, for the opening of a future worth living.

But wait, you ask, doesn't the Apocalypse itself—let's face it— reveal utter world destruction: "for the first heaven and the first earth had passed away . . ." (Rev. 21:1)?

2. O Clouds Unfold!

I do not, however, want to reveal the ending of the Apocalypse just yet. No suspense there, you might interject. That Last Book is all too easy to find, there at the Bible's end, performing its End Things. . . .

Yes. In general usage religious and secular, apocalypse signifies catastrophic termination: mere disclosure of closure. Self-designated Christian literalists still await the (literal) end of the world as transition to the certified heavenly reward for themselves. Popular interpretations of the New Testament's last book—their certainty recharged at every new breaking point of history—routinely perform the familiar narrative: that of a predestined and punitive world annihilation dictated (for our own good, of course) by the Divine Dictator. The world shuts down, and the New Jerusalem, read as heavenly reward for the chosen elect, "comes down."

Book closed. Along with time itself.

But contrary to general presumption and Christian literalism, John's letter literally, to the letter (Lat. *littera*), does *not* announce "the end of the world." It does depict a symbolically supercharged spiral of catastrophes, vividly amping up the destruction of a *particular* world: a specified global civilization and its planetary ecology. But neither the book nor its world ends there. In its conclusion—and this should build, not relieve, suspense—Revelation will construct an elaborate dream-architecture of radical urban and earth renewal.[5]

---

5. Chapter 7 will show that Revelation 21–22 portrays both urban

Still. Why now look for last chances in that archaic cloud of doom?

Perhaps first of all because the visions that make it up will not just drift away. The invocation of the language of apocalypse seems for now inescapable—and rent with contradiction. On the one hand, particularly in the United States, a deep evangelical legacy of literalist readings of the Apocalypse persists—despite the "Great Disappointment" of Jesus's failure to arrive on October 22, 1844, as predicted by the Millerites (later reorganized as the Seventh-day Adventists). New predictions of The End, usually more cautious in announcing precisely "the day and the hour," have continued to pour forth, endlessly. They have exercised a harrowing level of political influence, often veiled, and sometimes unveiled: as for example in Ronald Reagan's concurrence with an '80s fundamentalist expectation of imminent nuclear Armageddon. So the right-wing religio-political version of the A/apocalypse, in its opposition to public investment in a viable collective future, is hardly irrelevant to the decades that followed. Even when many pulses of American ideology were not overtly Armageddonesque.

At the same time, however, a very different history has long been fostered under the *other* wing. Christian millennialism has deployed Revelation to demand radical transformation.[6] The ancient prophetic hope of justice for the oppressed and care for the vulnerable was the origin of Jewish apocalyptic movements, and their

---

and rural ideals—the river, the tree(s) of life, etc.—that would have echoed with Greco-Roman visions of a largely rural utopia. See also Eric J. Gilchrest, *Revelation 21–22 in Light of Jewish and Greco-Roman Utopianism* (Boston: Brill, 2013).

6. For a brief rendition of the apocalyptic and revolutionary history of Revelation, see Catherine Keller, *Apocalypse Now and Then: A Feminist Guide to the End of the World* (Boston: Beacon, 1996; reprint, Minneapolis: Fortress Press, 2004), 17.

Christian heirs: "From first to last, and not merely in the epilogue, Christianity is eschatology, is hope." So pronounced the great theologian of hope Jürgen Moltmann. That tradition of "eschatology," misleadingly read as "doctrine of end things," is about a hope that is "revolutionizing and transforming the present."[7] *Eschatos* means not just "end" but "edge." This is no soft hope but an edgy demand. The vision of social transformation—for "the new song," "the new heaven and earth," "the New Jerusalem"—fired up Christian dissenting movements like the itinerant early Franciscans, the Radical Reformation and the German Peasant Revolt, the anti-establishment practices of the Quakers, the utopianisms of the Shakers, and the activism of the Social Gospel. And these took ever more secular and egalitarian form, fomenting the political revolutions of the modern epoch, democratic and socialist.

All along, a certain Christianity has stayed eschatologically tuned to the edges of the collective present. As Moltmann wrote decades later, anticipating our ecological future: "It is a crisis of life on this planet, a crisis so comprehensive and so irreversible that it cannot unjustly be described as apocalyptic. It is not a temporary crisis. . . . As far as we can judge, it is the beginning of a life and death struggle for creation on this earth."[8] And crucially, for any biblically sound eschatology, it is not that something new will "take the place of the old"; "it is the same 'old' itself which is going to be created anew."[9]

In the interest of reopening that history at the end of the millennium, I had tracked both the reactionary and the revolution-

---

7. Jürgen Moltmann, *Theology of Hope* (New York: Harper & Row, 1967), 16.

8. Jürgen Moltmann, *God in Creation: A New Theology of Creation and the Spirit of God*, trans. Margaret Kohl (Minneapolis: Fortress Press, 1993), xiii.

9. Jürgen Moltmann, *The Coming of God: Christian Eschatology* (Minneapolis: Fortress Press, 1996), 88.

ary wings of Revelation's effects in my *Apocalypse Now and Then*.[10] Yet in this new millennium I would not be returning to the topic but for the mounting chorus of voices secular, sober, and scientifically tuned who make use of the rhetoric of apocalypse. For instance, as I was drafting this segment, another headline pops up: "Chris Packham warns of ecological apocalypse in Britain." This English naturalist writes that "it's catastrophic and that's what we've forgotten. . . . Our generation is presiding over an ecological apocalypse and we've somehow or other normalised it."[11] Packham then describes the scene in a landscape he knows well, that of the rolling hills of the Cotswolds: "How many wildflowers can we see? None. Where's the pink of ragged robin? Where's the yellow of flag iris? The other colors are not there. It's not green and pleasant—it's green and unpleasant."

British readers immediately recognize the allusion to William Blake's "And did those feet in ancient time." It is a poem that ends thus:

> I will not cease from Mental Fight,
> Nor shall my Sword sleep in my hand:
> Till we have built Jerusalem,
> In England's green & pleasant Land.[12]

It is the building of the New Jerusalem to which this early modern deployment of the *constructive* potential of the Apocalypse

---

10. Keller, *Apocalypse Now and Then*, chap. 3, "Time: Temporizing Spaces." See also Ernst Bloch, *The Principle of Hope*, 3 vols.; trans. Neville Plaice, Stephen Plaice, and Paul Knight (Cambridge, MA: MIT Press, 1986).

11. Patrick Barkham, "Chris Packham Warns of 'Ecological Apocalypse' in Britain," *The Guardian* (June 11, 2018), theguardian.com.

12. William Blake, *Milton: A Poem in Two Books*, in *Milton: The Prophetic Books of William Blake*, ed. E. R. D. Maclagan and G. B. Russell (London: A. H. Bullen, 1907), xix.

refers: the greenly urban hope we will find in the final sign of the Book of Revelation.

That sword? Yes, the poetry has edge: it confronts the coal-filthy capitalism into which eighteenth-century England led the world. Regarding the already horrifying levels of mining and industrial pollution, Blake asks sarcastically: "And was Jerusalem builded here / Among these dark Satanic mills?" In his prophetic denunciation of the fossil-fueled assault on human and environmental health, the poet mobilizes—against the modern industrial revolution—the metaforce of apocalyptic revolution:

> Bring me my Bow of burning gold;
> Bring me my Arrows of desire
> Bring me my Spear: O clouds unfold!
> Bring me my chariot of fire![13]

The present book will not try to escape either that militant edge of desire or those darkly luminous clouds. O still unfold!

Packham was citing Blake to bemoan the reduction of our nonhuman universe to nature reserves, its remaining beauty "becoming like art installations." We enjoy the aesthetic exceptions and numb up to the rest. The "Satanic" becomes normal, and the apocalypse a mere shadow cast by fossil-fuel biz as usual. Yet shouldn't apocalypse name the *opposite* of the normal? For to normalize the civilization's ancient warning symbol is to disable its alarm—and therefore also its revolutionary potential. Catastrophe is then accepted as inevitable. Facing the mounting pattern of California's climate-driven wildfires, its governor announced "the new abnormal."[14] Similarly, Packham, who leads

---

13. Ibid.

14. "Prepare for the 'new abnormal.'" That was what California Governor Jerry Brown famously told reporters [in November 2018], commenting on the deadly wildfires that plagued the state that year—as

local activist endeavors, is mobilizing apocalyptic language to confront, not to normalize, catastrophe. The rhetoric of ecological apocalypse serves then as a wake-up call. Often to heed what seems so small: not a single butterfly in his garden this year, he noted. (Oh but I saw a monarch in mine. One.)

The small ripples into the shockingly large. A landmark study in Germany reported a 76 percent loss in total insect life. It was called the "Insect Armageddon"—without sarcasm, as unfortunately the research, conducted over a twenty-five–year period, was all too scientifically credible. "Insects make up about two-thirds of all life on Earth [but] there has been some kind of horrific decline."[15] The cause is not reducible to climate change. It is being attributed largely to extensive agricultural use of pesticides, which interact with warming in ways not yet fully understood. But this much we do understand: "We appear to be making vast tracts of land inhospitable to most forms of life, and are currently on course for ecological Armageddon. If we lose the insects then everything is going to collapse."[16] In more recent studies, the same

---

in each subsequent year. He was right. California's latest crisis builds on years of record-breaking droughts and heat waves. The rest of the world, too, has had more than its fair share of extreme weather in 2018. The *Lancet* Countdown on health and climate change announced that 157 million more people were exposed to heat wave events in 2017, compared with 2000. See David G. Victor, "Global Warming Will Happen Faster Than We Think," *Nature* (December 5, 2018).

15. Caspar A. Hallmann et al., "More Than 75 Percent Decline Over 27 Years in Total Flying Insect Biomass in Protected Areas," *PLOS ONE* 12, no. 10 (October 18, 2017), doi.org/10.1371/journal.pone.0185809; Damien Carrington, "Warning of 'Ecological Armageddon' after Dramatic Plunge in Insect Numbers," *The Guardian* (October 18, 2017), https://www.theguardian.com.

16. Evidence has been mounting that insect populations are under threat globally. For example, a 2014 study indicated a 45 percent decline in insect abundance on the majority of the worldwide monitored

pattern has been demonstrated in both Americas. Thus the cover
title of the far-from-alarmist *New York Times Magazine*: "The
Insect Apocalypse Is Here."[17] So sudden, so small. Almost unno-
ticed. Almost normalized. But making news.

Such apocalypses increasingly buzz through the rhetoric of
scientific reporting. Not of religious wingnuts. Going even smaller,
to the scene of the atom, we note the update of the Doomsday
Clock of the *Bulletin of Atomic Scientists*. "Using the imagery of
apocalypse (midnight)," it writes in a recent update that "the Bulletin of the Atomic Scientists Science and Security Board today
moves the Doomsday Clock 20 seconds closer to midnight—closer
to apocalypse than ever . . . the international security situation is
now more dangerous than it has ever been, even at the height of
the Cold War."[18] This is because along with nuclear danger, these
physicists now factor "cyber-enabled disinformation campaigns,"
along with the extreme perils of environmental break-down, particularly through global warming, into their calculations.[19] Thus

locations. See Rudolf Dirzo et al., "Defaunation in the Anthropocene,"
Science 345, no. 6195 (July 25, 2014): 401–6; Paula Kover, "Insect
'Armageddon': 5 Crucial Questions Answered," *Scientific American*
(October 30, 2017).

17. Brooke Jarvis, "The Insect Apocalypse Is Here," *The New York
Times Magazine* (November 27, 2018).

18. "Founded in 1945 by University of Chicago scientists who had
helped develop the first atomic weapons in the Manhattan Project, the
Bulletin of the Atomic Scientists created the Doomsday Clock two years
later, using the imagery of apocalypse (midnight) and the contemporary
idiom of nuclear explosion (countdown to zero) to convey threats to
humanity and the planet. The decision to move (or to leave in place) the
minute hand of the Doomsday Clock is made every year by the Bulletin's
Science and Security Board in consultation with its Board of Sponsors,
which includes thirteen Nobel laureates." See Science and Security
Board, "Closer Than Ever: It Is 100 Seconds to Midnight," *Bulletin of the
Atomic Scientists*, ed. John Mecklin (2020).

19. Dawn Stover, "How Many Hiroshimas Does It Take to Describe

they remind us of the entanglement of nonhuman ecology with human politics.

Fortunately, doom has never been a one-way clock. The hands sometimes move counterclockwise. As I write, a butterfly flutters by—a second one!—dancing counterdoom.

3. And Counting

Scientific and ecological secularizations of the apocalypse usually mean to denormalize doom. They signal the opposite of a determinist or a default inevitability: they are urgently invoking the still *evitable*. But the appeal of apocalypse remains charged with cultural contradiction. For instance, I once grabbed and purchased a book called *Trumpocalypse*, by Paul McGuire and Troy Anderson. As I'd coined that term in class the gloomy day after the 2016 election I presumed a sympathetic perspective.

The book does in opening discuss the Doomsday Clock, and it notes correctly that "most liberals and progressives fear Trump is emotionally unstable, impulsive, arrogant, narcissistic, and almost fascist-like in his political beliefs." Considering the "many complexities great leaders often have," and that Trump "had not led the life of a believer," it then asks: "Does Trump have a deep-seated Messiah complex, or is it possible that whatever his imperfections and flaws, he is being used by God in far more mysterious ways than we realize?"[20] Ah, the pivot. "Are

---

Climate Change?," *Bulletin of the Atomic Scientists* (September 26, 2013).

20. Paul McGuire and Troy Anderson, *Trumpocalypse: The End-Times President, a Battle against the Globalist Elite, and the Countdown to Armageddon* (New York: FaithWords, 2018), 10. The trend has continued, Hunter Bragg tells me, with the more recent memoir by Mark Taylor called the *Trump Prophecies*, published in 2017, in which God tells Taylor (a fireman with PTSD) that Trump is God's chosen

there ancient and contemporary prophecies that speak of the role of Trump and America in the last days?" Note that "prophecy" here is synonymous with "prediction." The authors go on to ask, rhetorically: "Do some of these prophecies foretell cataclysmic events in the not-too-distant future?" After all, "a 'political earthquake' swept Trump into office—halting eight years of a Marxist, leftwing presidency that divided the nation, eroded national sovereignty. . . ."[21]

The authors then follow Rev. Franklin Graham's declaration of the administration's "Christian revolution" with a revelation of the presidential codes (not the nuclear ones, I presume): this president counts as the "enigmatic figure who became seventy years, seven months, and seven days old on his first full day in the White House—January 21, 2017." As we can't get enough of the biblically certified seven, deemed the code of spiritual perfection (derived from the seven days of creation), a "destiny involving Israel" is now unveiled: "Israel was seventy-seven days old, seven hundred and seventy-seven days after Trump was born. Israel's seventieth birthday will arrive seven hundred days after Trump's seventieth birthday."[22]

I stop there, for if you aren't one of those old Obamarxists, you are surely already persuaded . . . that you want to pursue the seven chapters of *Facing Apocalypse* through each of their seven sections, in order to unseal seven signs lifted from Revelation and applied to the present crisis. For the present author, whose name is thrice seven letters (if you include my middle name), writes

---

candidate and will be to America what Netanyahu is to Israel. It's since been picked up and made into a movie called *The Trump Prophecy* (2018). Interestingly, but not at all surprisingly, Liberty University was involved in the movie-making process.

21. McGuire and Anderson, *Trumpocalypse*, 37, 39.
22. McGuire and Anderson, *Trumpocalypse*, 21.

these words on the seventh hour of the seventh day of the seventh month. . . .

4. Minding the Apocalypse

Or you might want to abandon the Apocalypse to those who have already solved and sold its mysteries: from the bestselling *Late Great Planet Earth* on through the *Left Behind* series, *The Babylon Code, Trumpocalypse*, and forward. Such updates were needed, as earth failed to get terminated, even with Hal Lindsey's flexible late-century timeline and pious association with President Reagan, nuclear codes in hand.

We will keep seeing updates of all kinds. So we may no more be able to abandon the Apocalypse than we can leave planet Earth. For John's metaphors now come wrapped in the trials and tribulations of "all of the inhabitants of the earth" (Rev. 12:12; 13:8). Some more than others. And as cli-fi and cli-sci illustrate, ever more irreversible doom looms, unless the "Satanic mills" of the economic order cease rather soon to fuel the political ecology of Armageddon. No doubt figures of sword-tongue, dragon, beasts, great whore, warrior messiah and friends have added fuel to the fires. So we might cease to invest in them the energy of our interest (and stop reading this book). But as that won't make them go away, we might want instead to face them. To make their faces as conscious as possible—as one grapples with a bad dream so that it will not keep recurring. But then everything depends upon our interpretation. Which is to say, how we read its overread and over-heated metaforce.

Let us briefly consider four very different apocalypse-reading strategies. Only the fourth will be advanced in this book, but it cannot launch without a grasp of the first three.

The most common reading is this: we view the ancient images

through the lens of *biblical prediction*. Then the wildly metaphoric imaginary of the Apocalypse is captured and reduced to a code for reading the future. The future is already "known" by God, preset in the changeless present of "His" omnipotence. The symbols are controlled by this literalism of presumptive prediction. It remains denialist as to the possibility that humans are changing anything as big as earth's climate, which was "intelligently designed" in those (literal) seven days. This predictive literalism is indifferent to an older and longer-term earth, one later and maybe greater than ours. For the planet is predetermined for destruction soon, very soon—though always a bit later. This reading knows no realm of human responsibility between the multiple peoples, traditions and ways of the earth, let alone between normalcy and The End.

The second lens seems like the very opposite of endtime prediction: a modern *"can do" optimism*. Its spirit of technological progress, economic growth, and individual freedom pervades white U.S. culture, presenting itself as the only alternative to pessimism. It trusts human exceptionalism to rescue us from doom and gloom: scientific or religious. And yet a form of the capitalist confidence has folded itself into right-wing versions of Christianity, fueling the opposition of the religious right to climate science for decades. With funding from the Koch brothers (whose fortune welled up first from crude oil) the influential Cornwall Alliance for the Stewardship of Creation has worked against any "convincing scientific evidence that human contribution to greenhouse gases is causing dangerous global warming."[23] It well exemplifies the collusion of fundamentalist denialism and capitalist optimism.

---

23. "Evangelical Declaration on Global Warming," *Cornwall Alliance for the Stewardship of Creation* (May 1, 2009).

The third: despising such fundamentalist irresponsibility yet mirroring it in reverse, apocalypse can sink into a *pacifying nihilism*. It claims to have "grown honest." Critical attention to the intractable mechanisms of social injustice, to new surges of white nationalism, to irreversible environmental destruction *can* lead to anger and action. But to act takes some feeling that your actions can just possibly make a difference: not certainty, not optimism, but hope. Yet—all too understandably—a now-fashionable hopelessness is normalizing pessimism. It can take credible intellectual, even theological form. Mostly, however, it yields a casual catastrophism, vaguely glamorized as radical, with a shrug of "why bother." In its detachment from the world, such nihilism functions in effect like the flip side of denialism.

The fourth reading of the apocalypse resists both optimistic denialism and pessimistic nihilism. At the same time it avoids both the literalizations and the dismissals of the biblical Apocalypse. Within Christianity it drives a spectrum of liberation and ecological theologies. It readily allies itself to secular movements for transformation (e.g., Black Lives Matter, Extinction Rebellion, Greta Thunberg's strikes for a future). Beyond the mirror play of denialism and nihilism, this reading will evince an *apocalyptic mindfulness*. Its hope cannot cut free of its own doubt. It recognizes itself as grasping at effectual language, and sometimes at straws.[24] It presses beyond flat factualities, secular or fundamentalist; and beyond despairing surrender. It faces the unspeakable catastrophes that may become inevitable *if* we do not speak. If we glide into apocalyptic normalization.

---

24. Such hope hopes against whole histories of false hopes. "Hope is the risky business of calling for the coming of what we cannot see coming, of saying yes to the future, where nothing is guaranteed." John D. Caputo, *Hoping against Hope: Confessions of a Postmodern Pilgrim* (Minneapolis: Fortress, 2015), 199.

The *de*normalization of the Apocalypse requires that we *mind* its metaphors. "To mind" carries the meaning of being bothered, concerned, and at the same time of practicing a heightened, even meditative, attention. That attention flows from the reading of shared nightmares, shared dreams. How else can we mind—face—the danger and help activate response—ability? Perhaps not in dissociation from challenging affects like fear, shame, despair, and doubt, but as a liberating and therefore activating attention. Such responsibility wants of us both contemplative and activist activations.

In the interest of this fourth way, I invite the reader into direct touch with a few ancient faces of the Apocalypse: figures embedded in scenes that work in the present like collective dreams, like planetary nightmares. The old text is itself charged with both hope and with trauma. Its metaphors have been cultural forces for nearly two thousand years, getting realized mindfully or mindlessly, in healing or in hatred. Clouds, seas, lambs, many-horned beasts, imperial prostitute, jeweled cities—these signs certainly operate in the depths of what has been called the collective unconscious. Such ancient signs are not timeless but *timeful*—overcharged with historical enactment, expectation, disappointment. They operate also in the widths of what has been called the political unconscious.[25] They root in configurations of collective experience deeper and more multiple than any individual mind can reach. They transmit layers of our entanglement with each other, of our earthly ancestry human and otherwise, into a process moving both faster and slower than we ever quite grasp.

---

25. Fredric Jameson, *The Political Unconscious: Narrative as a Socially Symbolic Act* (Ithaca, NY: Cornell University Press, 1981). On C. G. Jung's very different "collective unconscious," see Catherine Keller, *From a Broken Web: Separation, Sexism, and Self* (Boston: Beacon Press, 1986). While I share the reading of certain signs and symbols as shared at a collective and largely imperceptible depth, I do not name the signs "archetypes," which carry an aura of timeless and universal truth.

These self-renewing old metaphors, these metaforces, operate across multiple temporal variations of spiritual and secular power. To dismiss or repress them is only to lose track of them. Then they get acted out unconsciously, and all the more dangerously. For individuals or groups unconscious of their own apocalyptic affect readily project it onto some alien, some Other. This justifies an affect of righteous antagonism—and the violence it sanctions.

Minding the apocalypse does not require becoming an expert on the Book of Revelation, or on any of the myriad historical movements it spawned. It is not about being this or that sort of Christian, or about being religious at all. It will, however, help us each to face what we fear with more courage (that word coming from the French *coeur*, "heart"). In taking heart there pulses a solidarity of unexpected possibility. It guarantees no happy ending. But it does enhance the uncertain chance of better outcomes. It is for the sake of that chance that we practice, in and beyond this reading, apocalyptic mindfulness.

5. Bronze and Breasted

In the middle of the lampstands was someone who looked like a human being. He wore a robe that stretched down to his feet and had a gold sash wrapped around his chest. His head and hair were white as white wool—like snow— and his eyes were like a flame of fire. His feet were like shining bronze, refined as in a furnace, and his voice was like the sound of rushing water. He held seven stars in his right hand, and from his mouth came a sharp two-edged sword. (Rev. 1:9–16, K)

The dreamreading. It has already begun: our own, and also John's. "Look! He is coming with the clouds...." The cloud is a saturated symbol. It is not just one person's raw vision. John's Apocalypse comes packed with citations of earlier prophets. So in his first chapter John is citing, as he often does, the second-century BCE Book of Daniel: "I saw one like a human being coming with the clouds of heaven" (Dan. 7:13). Such clouds appear also in the Gospel of Matthew, rough contemporary of the Apocalypse, as it narrates the messianic event of Yeshuah (later transliterated as "Jesus") meeting Moses and Elijah for a powwow on a mountaintop. Then "suddenly a bright cloud overshadowed them" (Matt. 17:5). Peter is stunned into incoherent babbling. That dreamscene, called the transfiguration, is itself a refiguration of Moses's ancient rendezvous atop Mt. Sinai with the Nameless One "in a dense cloud" (Exod. 19:9).

The trail of clouds comes dense with history and possibility, irreducible to a single meaning. It brings a prophecy tinged with mysticism—not prediction, not knowing the future, not the certitude of later religious know-it-alls. Here we return to gather that cloud's prophetic metaforce from the first sign of John's apocalypse. The one coming with the clouds of vision is, in the original, "someone who looked like a human being."[26] The phrase is a citation of Daniel. John does not identify the human-like figure as "Jesus" or "Christ." Yet his original Greek gets routinely translated into the familiar title "Son of Man." Hear how that christological simplification eliminates the messianic mysteriousness that John conveys? The clouds have a political as well as a spiritual charge. For Jesus and his first-century followers, the clouds cover a new political context: It is no longer the Babylonian and Persian empires of Daniel, but the new global imperium of Rome.

In our context (postimperial? neoimperial? nationalist? global?)

---

26. Craig R. Koester, *Revelation: A New Translation with Introduction and Commentary*, Anchor Bible (New Haven: Yale University Press, 2014), 13.

what do the clouds unfold? What cumulus of meaning, what cumulative force of history, might be covering us now?

I think we cannot even see its textual face unless we help the vision defamiliarize itself: first of all to get free of an image so flat, so hard, so harshly clarified by centuries of overuse that cliché has replaced cloud. To better mind its "someone who looked like a human" we might ask: what might it, might he, might they look like at this moment?

"His head and his hair were white as white wool, white as snow. . . . His feet were like shining bronze, refined as in a furnace, and his voice was like the sound of many waters" (1:14ff.). But in what sense is the head white? Is this the "messianic white man" who presides—so normally—over recent centuries of Christian racial supremacism? "The White Masculine as imperial Man," writes J. Kameron Carter, "was tied to his assuming a messianic and mediatory role in the world."[27] Ironically, when the figure's skin color is mentioned in the same biblical passage, it is "like burnished bronze"—not copper, not the color of a golf-course tan, but a glowing brown. Of course it emanates from a context where there existed nothing like the modern European notion of race, nothing like the identification of ethnicity by skin color. The skin of this "someone" stands out in enigmatic contrast to the shock of white wooly hair, as of one prematurely aged. The reverse of our standard picture of the white Jesus with dark hair, this one is white haired and dark skinned.

Some renditions of the figure come closer to the radical spirit of John than others. Hear, for instance, *Black Messiah*, the album of singer, songwriter, and multi-instrumentalist D'Angelo. It opens

---

27. J. Kameron Carter, "Between W. E. B. Du Bois and Karl Barth: The Problem of Modern Political Theology," in *Race and Political Theology*, ed. Vincent W. Lloyd (Stanford, CA: Stanford University Press, 2012), 89.

with an audio sample of Black Panther Party chairman Khalid Abdul Muhammad: "When I say Jesus, I'm not talking about some blond-haired, blue-eyed, pale-skinned, buttermilk complexion cracker Christ. I'm talking about the Jesus of the Bible, with hair like lamb's wool. I'm talking about that good hair, I'm talking about that nappy hair."[28] African American religion hosts a potent subculture of revolutionary Apocalypse, with its lamb-haired messiah and his "militant grace."[29]

In the turbulent cloud another kind of revelation was always brewing, alien to the pale male Lord who became the Christian norm. His denormalizations do not stop with race. In the same scene the figure wears a white robe, with "a golden sash over the *mastoi*," usually translated tamely as "chest" (1:3). But the Greek word *mastoi* signifies women's breasts.[30] Oddly it is the King James translation that maintains the trace of the unexpected gender: "Girt about the paps with a golden girdle."[31] No more than John himself would the seventeenth-century translators have intended

---

28. D'Angelo and the Vanguard, *1000 Deaths* (RCA Records, 2014). D'Angelo, the son of a Pentecostalist minister, knows well and is not literalizing the Book of Revelation. Thanks to O'neil Van Horn, who shared this source with me "in all its funky glory."

29. Philip G. Zeigler, *Militant Grace: The Apocalyptic Turn and the Future of Christian Theology* (Grand Rapids, MI: Baker Academic, 2018); Brian K. Blount, *Can I Get a Witness? Reading Revelation through African American Culture* (Louisville, KY: Westminster John Knox Press, 2005).

30. I suddenly really saw the old cross my birthfather Milton Cohen brought back as an antique from Mexico in the late 1940s. An impious artist, he must have admired the evident femininity of the crucified Jesus's breasts.

31. "Paps" referred in medieval English to women's breasts or to breast milk (Rev. 1:13). Perhaps it is just a coincidence that King James was also known as "Queen James" and understood by multiple contemporaries to favor men as sexual partners.

to feminize, let alone to queer, the Messiah. Metaforce exceeds intention.

The breasted messianic one now thrusts forth his (their) tongue: "he held seven stars in his right hand, and from his mouth came a sharp two-edged sword" (1:16a). In contrast to the expected "celestial superwarrior," Stephen Moore finds here "the epiphany of the risen Christ as celestial androgyne." This leading scholar of the Apocalypse reads the cloud with dissident precision: "the God of Revelation is a hypermasculine God. But masculinity in excess tends to teeter over inexorably into its opposite." Indeed, in the logic of dreams opposites tend to coincide in contradiction or in compensation. "The intersexed body of Jesus Christ in Revelation's inaugural vision may be read as a call to consequential decisions about what a person is or may be, and hence a call for justice of the most fundamental kind—but a call that Revelation itself fails to heed consistently."[32]

Apocalyptic mindfulness keeps us tuned to the messianic call across sex, across race, across systems of injustice—and its repeated twist into its pious opposite. Dreamreading John's vision-parody of social norms in his context may reveal something also about ourselves. And about who—she, he, they, it—calls. What is cutting through. From within ourselves. From beyond ourselves.

6. Rocky Animation

At once I was in the spirit, and there in heaven stood a throne! And the one seated there looks like jasper and carnelian, and around the throne is a rainbow that looks like an emerald. Around the throne are twenty-four thrones, and seated on the thrones are twenty-four elders, dressed

---

32. Stephen D. Moore, *Untold Tales from the Book of Revelation: Sex and Gender, Empire and Ecology* (Atlanta, GA: SBL Press, 2014), 97, 151.

in white robes, with golden crowns on their heads. Coming from the throne are flashes of lightning, and rumblings and peals of thunder . . . and in front of the throne there is something like a sea of glass, like crystal. (Rev. 4:2–6)

The two-edged sword-tongue protrudes as prophecy, as cutting parody of Power. Indeed what strong social transformation happens without sharp language and fierce insistence? Of course such a double edge may turn on allies as well as enemies. If the cloud-coded signs keep us feeling the tensions, the internal and even intersexed ambiguities of the text, we will also mind its militancy—particularly when we face "the Weaponized Word," the sixth of our seven signs. But the point will not be to project back onto a two-thousand-year-old text recent antiracist, ecological, or queer struggles. Let us instead mind the possibilities already tipping this sharp tongue: this S/Word.

One may always normalize the cloud-figure as simply "Jesus Christ." Yet in the text that identification remains unspoken. The figure's most consistent textual embodiment is hinted at in the cloud-white afro. Soon it will morph into a lamb. In the meantime this bronze-skinned wooly-headed sword-tongued androgyne bearing a bouquet of stars seems not even to speak human language: "his voice was like the sound of many waters." Like a dark cloud's thunderous rain, like rivers singing, like oceans roaring? If the Book of Revelation opens with the sound of waters, it then courses through mounting hydro-traumas, and streams finally into the "water of life." What is a cloud, after all, but condensed water?

In the first chapters John is addressing his letter to several (seven of course) congregations. His introductory messaging is itself double-edged: sometimes warm praise, sometimes judgment, and in the worst case, a sexist denunciation of the spiritual leader he calls, as though spitting at her unveiled body, "Jezebel." Only after those messages does the vision pick up again, to offer the content of the letter. Then John is again "in the spirit," in an altered state, dreamreading, dreamreadable. We find ourselves invited through a "door that had been opened in heaven"—dis/ closure, after all. Then the imagery kaleidoscopes into twenty-four elder-occupied thrones surrounding a central one, upon which sits *not* a crowned and bearded elder male. Instead we see a being that "looked like jasper and carnelian, and around the throne a rainbow that looked like an emerald. . . ."

An all-green rainbow? Let us not project there a symbolic Oz of eco-hope. What comes into focus on the throne sparkles across the color spectrum: "Jasper referred to precious stones ranging from green to blue, purple to rose. . . . Carnelian was a reddish stone, which suggests that God's presence had a fiery radiance as in Ezekiel 1:27."[33] No anthropomorphic, let alone white, king with begemmed crown: this God does not look human(ish)—but like two gems. The throne room itself is full of life, elders, spirits, creatures. And radiating at its core, as far from human as imaginable, sits this (double) Rock of Ages—sparkling and stony, multifaceted and multicolored, surrounded by "a sea of glass, crystal. Inhumanly dazzling, does its crystallization refract the full spectrum of the creation?

In a sudden close-up appear—in hallucinatory contrast to the inorganic ultimate—"four living creatures that were covered with eyes on the front and on the back" (Rev. 4:7, K). So these omni-ocular organisms stand in the immediate circle of the throne—as though providing eyes for the faceless double-gem. But they are distinctly themselves:

> The first living creature was like a lion, the second living creature was like an ox, the third living creature had a face like a human being, and the fourth living creature was like an eagle in flight. (Rev. 4:8, K)

33. Koester, *Revelation*, 360.

Reminiscent of the zoomorphic totems of indigenous peoples, these images are all "like," not identical with, their animals. They are supercharged vision-creatures: each of the four have six wings and "are full of eyes all around and inside" (Rev. 4:8). Those starry eyes—both covering and lining the creatures—never close for sleep, "day and night." John seems here to redream visions of earlier prophets. In Isaiah, the throne is surrounded by similarly six-winged creatures.[34] In Ezekiel, the four creatures appear, but it is the four wheels of God's chariot that are rimmed in eyes. That vehicle of change returns millennia later as the inspiration of the African American spiritual "Ezekiel Saw 'de Wheel,'" as well as the abolitionist song, "Swing Low, Sweet Chariot."

We might dreamread John's creatures thus: the vision hints at the polymorphic diversity of the creation.[35] Their eyes front and back, inside and out, open our eyes (*apokalypsis*) to something largely unseen about the universe: that the living creation, alive in and through its creatures, is wide-eyed with awareness. Somehow that strange multiocularity is God's own. The creatures circle the deity, who without the bodies and eyes might be just a cold pair of big stones. Also the placement of the humanoid as mere third of four animals cannot be an accident. Might it flash a cosmic corrective to the anthropocentrism that mistakes our species' talent

---

34. "Seraphs were in attendance above him; each had six wings: with two they covered their faces, and with two they covered their feet, and with two they flew" (Is. 6:2). This image recurs in Jewish Merkabah mysticism.

35. Already for the theologian Irenaeus in the century following John, the four creatures became an allegory of the four Gospels. This symbolization stuck right through the Reformation. While such rendition remains fair game, the author of the Apocalypse refers to no "Gospels," which became written books during the same period he was writing. Also the allegory of course represses the gaminess of the animal element, with its implicit subversion of human exceptionalism.

(our creation "in the image of God") with limitless supremacy? That misreads human difference as absolute exception?

John of Patmos could not have known where that human exceptionalism would take the planet, a couple millennia hence. No. But we will have reason to suspect he had a dark clue. And so in advance of his tormented visions of the great spiral of damage to all the creatures of the planet, a surreal glimpse of divine, human, and nonhuman synergy registers. The God-gems are enveloped by the four creatures, as the inorganic center of their organisms.[36]

In other words the mandala of the throne room centers a relation of the divine and the creaturely: the relation is one of simultaneous difference and inseparability. This entangled difference can be dubbed "divinanimality"—a neologism of the philosopher Jacques Derrida's late work, *This Animal That Therefore I Am*. Derrida found there is no redress of the deadly animal/human dualism of modernity without circling back through theology and its absolute animal/divine divide.[37] Our ecological imbalance, with its now monstrously accelerating animal extinctions, presumes those dualisms. Once we in the West learned to abstract and extract an immaterial, timeless Creator from the matter of creation, we could then project onto God our delusion of sepa-

---

36. A leading commentator, Craig R. Koester, puts it more traditionally: "God's entourage reflects his character . . . arranged in concentric circles that show the harmony of creation." See Koester, *Revelation*, 117.

37. Jacques Derrida, *The Animal That Therefore I Am*, ed. Marie-Louise Mallet; trans. David Wills (New York: Fordham University Press, 2008). Derrida's title is a parody of Descartes's supremely anthropocentric "I think, therefore I am." For a transdisciplinary engagement of the divine/animal/human question, see Stephen D. Moore, ed., *Divinanimality: Animal Theory, Creaturely Theology* (New York: Fordham University Press, 2014). Drew Transdisciplinary Theological Colloquium Series.

ration from our own animality, our animate materiality. In the divinanimality at the heart of the apocalyptic throne room some other animacy, more ancient than Judaism, wordlessly watches. John is not *predicting* the Sixth Great Extinction.[38] But he may, as we will soon see, be *prophesying* it.

In the meantime, we hear a vast chorus singing to the Rock of all ages, not timeless but of all times: the one "who was, and who is, and who is to come" (Rev. 4:8). It holds in one hand "a scroll, written on the inside and the back, sealed with seven seals" (Rev. 5:1). Then an angelic solo: "Who is worthy to open the scroll and break its seals?" And the answer seems to be: "No one. . . ."

Devastated at this illegibility, poor textocentric John "wept and wept. . . ." The suspense builds. An elder now reassures him: "Stop weeping. You see, the Lion of the tribe of Judah, the Root of David has conquered, so that he can open the scroll and its seven seals" (Rev. 5:5). There could be no clearer sign than this animal meta-force: it heralds the Davidic *maschiach*, the anointed.[39] Though the Bible never, contrary to common Christian usage, speaks of a "Second Coming," this messianic coming will not be the first, as it seems he—already—"has conquered."

The sovereign Lion has been announced.

7. And Instead of the Lion

There enters into the intimate space "between the throne and the four living creatures. . . . A Lamb, standing as one who had been slain" (Rev. 5:6, K). Cinematically, the irony tenses with drama: the expectation of a proud symbol of power is flipped, thwarted,

---

38. Elizabeth Kolbert, *The Sixth Extinction: An Unnatural History* (New York: Henry Holt, 2014).

39. "The anointed" is the translation of Hebrew *maschiach*, rendered in English "messiah," the one anointed with oil in the tradition of the coronation of Israel's kings.

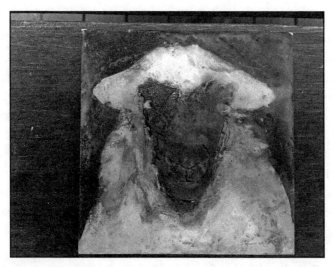

Jan Harrison, *The Tiny Ewe*, encaustic pastel on wood, 2008.

mocked by the materialization of the mildest of creatures, a sheep. Worse, a lamb, i.e., a baby sheep: a lamb.[40] A weird one with "seven eyes and seven horns." Worst, a slaughtered lamb. How does a slaughtered creature even stand? It seems that the little lamb bears a bloody trauma that cannot be washed off.

Before your mind's eye, however, there may already have popped up—like cartoon animation—the icon of the jaunty sheep carrying a small cross, no blood on his white coat. Over the centuries the normalization of the crucifixion as divinely directed sacrifice has washed away the honest gore of the Apocalypse. But in Mussolini's fascist secularization—tweeted eighty years later as a "good quote"—the weak lamb is dismissed: "I'd rather live a day as a lion than a hundred years as a lamb."[41]

---

40. The Greek word here is *arnion*, diminutive of *aren*, "sheep."

41. Dylan Stableford, "Donald Trump on Retweeting Mussolini: 'It's a Very Good Quote,'" *Yahoo! News*, February 18, 2016.

In the vision the lamb appears from within the wooly cloud. Yet commentators rarely note the fluffy continuity between the initial cloud, the nappy haired, breasted humanoid sticking out tongue-sword—and the full materialization of their white hair in the form of the lamb. Just too far from any lionesque sovereignty? Well, this isn't *literally* a lamb, you may say. And I say, well, to the *letter* of John's letter it is indeed a bloodied lamb, one with seven eyes, horns, spirits: yet another strange multi-ocular and -horned creature. Since John will prophesy vast nonhuman losses, let us not lose the cloud-trail of this creature's messianic animality. For it is only this Lamb who can break the seven seals of the scroll.

The Lamb opens the first seal, the first of the four creatures says, "Come!" and the first of the four horses gallops forth, white, its rider "crowned and conquering": the colonizing force of empire. The Armageddonesque disclosure continues: the red horse, the peace-breaker and instigator of human slaughter, encodes the violence of the *pax romana*. On the black horse, the rider bears scales: a sudden voice announces "a quart of wheat for a day's pay, and three quarts of barley for a day's pay, but do not damage the olive oil and the wine!" No voiceover accompanies the other horses. Why such material details? Because, it seems, these grainy images register in any currency of that time: unlivable pay, slave wages—while olive oil and wine were luxury products of Mediterranean trade. The voice in other words is revealing economic injustice. And last: the pale green horse gallops in, whose rider will "kill with sword, famine, and pestilence, and the wild animals of the earth" (Rev. 6:8). Unlike the first three, this sickly green one delivers torment by the nonhuman.

The Four Horsemen of the Apocalypse appear ever updatable. Albrecht Dürer's five-hundred-year-old woodcut, part of his famous Apocalypse series, seems to dreamread the unprecedented levels of slaughter that the Thirty Years' War between Protestants and Catholics would soon unleash. "What are the four horsemen of the apocalypse so pissed about?" Mark Vonnegut asks. "What situation could possibly be made better by unleashing war, pestilence, famine, and death?"[42] The equestrian quartet gallops through endless political applications: "Trump Apocalypse Watch" put his image atop each horse in dread of the 2016 election.[43] On the other wing, one spots *Obama's Four Horsemen: The Disasters Unleashed by Obama's Reelection.*[44] The right, of course, dominates, with fundamentalist blogs applauding the equine destruction as the direct work of Christ: "The gospel goes out conquering; it causes division; those who resist the gospel suffer famine; ultimately, those who resist the gospel are killed by sword, famine, and pestilence."[45] The Book of Revelation will be ever readable as justification of Christian violence. That is one strong reason we *mind* the text. *Apocalypse is not gospel.* But neither does it celebrate the horrors it curates.

But the last, pale green horse held a rider of death
A disease of pandemic was spread by its breath

---

42. Mark Vonnegut, *Just Like Someone without Mental Illness Only More So: A Memoir* (New York: Bantam Books, 2011), 164.

43. "The Trump Apocalypse Watch was a subjective daily estimate, using a scale of one to four horsemen, of how likely it was that Donald Trump would be elected president, thus triggering an apocalypse in which we all die." See Ben Mathis-Lilley, "The Last Trump Apocalypse Watch," *Slate* (November 9, 2016).

44. David Harsanyi, *Obama's Four Horsemen: The Disasters Unleashed by Obama's Reelection* (Washington, DC: Regnery Publishing, 2013).

45. Peter Leithart, "Horsemen of the Apocalypse," *Patheos* (July 9, 2018).

The legions of Hades with violence they seethed
From oppression the people could no longer breathe.

Rev. K. Karpen[46]

I was finishing the present book when the Fourth Horseman
came riding back round the world. In context, John is expanding
the Exodus plagues unleashed on Egypt a thousand years before
him to a scale of pestilence unknown in his time. The history of
pandemics proper begins only after John's death, with the Anto-
nine Plague of 165 CE. One might read him as foreseeing that one,
which took out 5 million people, including much of the Roman
Army. Pestilence has many times since turned pandemic and
returned—along with sightings of the pale green horse. At this
moment, feeding "Covid-19 book of Revelation" into the Google
search engine yields almost forty million results. That, writes
Stephen Moore, "is what Revelation is for, this is what Revelation
does. This is the default function of this disaster-voracious book
in a time of global crisis. Specifically, for hundreds of millions of
Christians worldwide, Revelation is subsuming the infra-agential
activity of submicroscopic suborganisms under the supra-agential
activity of a yet more invisible and more inscrutable divine being,
thereby transforming a time of pandemic into a time of plague."[47]

Not that the inorganic Rock sent the coronavirus, this crea-

---

46. I thank Rev. K. Karpen, who wrote the lyrics of this hymn (to
be sung to the tune of "How Firm a Foundation") for a service at St.
Paul and St. Andrew United Methodist Church, July 26, 2020. Here is
the final stanza: "These four riders that John saw creating upheaval / In
his dream-like disclosure of systemic evil / We can view in our current
world turbulent trauma / Bringing woe, lamentation, resistance and
drama." See K. Karpen, "The Uncovering," St. Paul & St. Andrew United
Methodist Church, New York, NY (July 26, 2020).

47. Stephen D. Moore, "Beastly Boasts and Apocalyptic Affects:
Reading Revelation in a Time of Trump and a Time of Plague," *Religions*
11, no. 7 (2020): 346.

ture crossing the boundary between nonlife and life. It did not come crowned with a teaching mission. It does, however, reveal the elemental interdependence of humans not just with each other across the planet, but with nonhuman others—right down to the microscopic level.

What does pestilence share with the fourth horseman's other nonhuman offerings—hunger and animal attacks? Does the prophecy face into (not predict) varieties of deadly payback by the nonhuman, against a species that exploits and ignores the nonhuman? Matter strikes back? The pale green meta-horse does snort a suggestive anachronism: hunger and food insecurity rose exponentially in 2020 with economically degraded and racially marked U.S. populations, those most vulnerable also to the virus. Wild animals? That fear dates the text. And yet the likeliest origin of Covid-19 remains transmission from wild animals (probably bats) delivering the virus.[48] Human disregard for nonhumans and their habitats has long boded ill. Therefore many scientists recognize in the coronavirus not a mere human but an ecological disease.[49]

See the pale green blur eerily into the fading green of the planet itself?

The fifth and sixth seals then break, exposing mass martyrdoms and a shaking, quaking earth. I will spare you the details. The "sky vanishes like a scroll rolling up"—as though to close the book on earth's history. But stay with it . . . the Lamb's scroll unfurls further.

In the cloud had appeared from the mouth of the human(ish) Messiah a "sharp, two-edged sword." The cloud shapeshifts into

---

48. Smriti Mallapaty, "Wildlife Trade Should Be Focus of Pandemic Origin Investigations," *Nature* 583, no. 7816 (July 16, 2020): 344.

49. Catherine Keller, "The Gallop of the Pale Green Horse: Pandemic, Pandemonium, and Panentheism," in *Pandemic, Economy, Theology*, ed. Alexander J. B. Hampton (New York: Routledge, 2020).

a Lamb who will remain speechless for the rest of the book. This Lamb, we read, "will be their shepherd." Hardly a sheepish sheep! He will "guide them to springs of the water of life. . . ." If the shepherd-sheep embodies leadership, it is not that of a controlling power, but—in a disarming dream-twist toward nonviolence—of a vulnerability beyond language. No Lion who rules but a Lamb who shepherds. Tongue in cloud.

As the next chapter opens, the silence of this Lamb stretches into cosmic suspense. In the ancient future of our present: what is coming unsealed?

"O clouds unfold."

2

Mourning Bird
Burning Trees, Poisoned Seas

When the Lamb opened the seventh seal, there was silence in heaven for about half an hour.

—Revelation 8:1

> ... *perhaps a huge silence*
> *might interrupt this sadness*
> *of never understanding ourselves*
> *and of threatening ourselves with death.*
> *Perhaps the earth can teach us*
> *As when everything seems dead*
> *And later proves to be alive.*
> *—Pablo Neruda, "Keeping Quiet"*

1. Blasts of Ecoapocalypse

The seventh seal. Does that phrase still trigger the image of Max von Sydow, all existential intensity, playing chess with Death? In Ingmar Bergman's great 1957 film *The Seventh Seal*, the medieval knight has returned from the Crusades, disillusioned, only to find Sweden devastated by the plague. In the epoch of Cold War after

Albrecht Dürer, *The Four Horsemen of the Apocalypse*, 1497/98, woodcut, collection of the Metropolitan Museum of Art, New York.

the U.S. atomic bombings of Hiroshima and Nagasaki, Bergman seems to have been musing on nuclear doom. His knight reads Revelation's silence in heaven as the silence of God.

In the ancient cinematics of John's Apocalypse, all four horsemen, spreading annihilation through power, violence, greed, and pandemic, have already ridden. Neither the gem God nor bloodied Lamb has said a word. The breaking of that seventh seal—followed by the great silence "for about half an hour"— dramatically heightens the suspense. The silence is held by the creatures, angels, enthroned elders, saints, gems and all: the crowd of celestial metaforces within the cloud of the unspeakable.

A silence of dark unknowing? Of divine indifference, mere absence, feared inexistence? Or of cosmic grief? False hopes and distracting fears are quieted in an awe-full preparation for what is to be revealed. In a practice of apocalyptic mindfulness.

Might we hold that silence now?

After the pause, seven angelic trumpeters step up. With brassy flourish, the first one blows, "and there came hail and fire, mixed with blood, and they were hurled to the earth; and a third of the earth was burned up, and a third of the trees were burned up, and all green grass was burned up" (Rev. 8:7).

Do you flash to fires raging across the twenty-first-century planet? Isn't that California, with its wildfire seasons now bearing "historic levels of death and destruction"?[1] Farther south, an archbishop, no fundamentalist, warns that the burning of the Amazon is "a true apocalypse."[2] Yet farther south, Australia—more than 20 percent of its forests burnt in this summer's bushfires.[3] And then wildfires leap weirdly north, to the unprecedentedly warmed Arctic Circle. No natural cycle of fire and renewal, these infernos devour hundreds of billions of trees.

At this point in John's vision, a third of the earth, of the trees, were burned up. At this point in our history, approximately half

---

1. Lauren Tierney, "The Grim Scope of 2017's California Wildfire Season Is Now Clear. The Danger's Not Over," *Washington Post* (January 4, 2018).

2. Archbishop Erwin Kräutler, quoted in Jonathan Watts and Harriet Sherwood, "Amazon Fires Are 'True Apocalypse,' Says Brazilian Archbishop," *The Guardian* (September 5, 2019).

3. Lisa Cox, "'Unprecedented' Globally: More Than 20% of Australia's Forests Burnt in Bushfires," *The Guardian* (February 24, 2020).

of the trees of the earth are gone, lost to flames and deforesta-
tions, infestations and droughts, on an overheating planet.[4] The
quiet trees. They not only support our breath with their oxygen
production but draw down deadly excess carbon from our atmosphere. Can there be a more vicious circle: global warming fueling fires that kill forests that counteract fossil fuel emissions that
drive global warming? Another name for the Anthropocene has
been coined—the "Pyrocene," the "Fire Age." Unaccompanied by
angelic trumpet, the prolific scholar of fires Steve Pyne announces
"a harbinger of things to come. Don't ignore the warning."[5]

The second trumpet blasts: "something like a great mountain,
burning with fire, was thrown into the sea. A third of the sea
became blood, and a third of the living creatures in the sea died."

Is it some kind of eco-fundamentalist projection to see ourselves darkly mirrored in the waves of that ancient future? With
massive die-offs of fish populations, with starving whales? And I
only recently learned of the threat that the warming of the waters
poses through ocean acidification to the phytoplankton at the
bottom of the food chain—and therefore to all of us breathers.
The phytoplankton produce the oxygen not just for the sea but
for *more than half* the air that we breathe.[6] Acidification seems

---

4. Christian Nunez, "Deforestation Explained," *National Geographic*
(February 7, 2019).

5. Steve Pyne, "The Australian Fires Are a Harbinger of Things
to Come. Don't Ignore Their Warning," *The Guardian* (January 7,
2020). See also Stephen J. Pyne, *Between Two Fires: A Fire History of
Contemporary America* (Tucson: University of Arizona Press, 2015);
and *To the Last Smoke: An Anthology* (Tucson: University of Arizona
Press, 2020).

6. As oceanographers tells us, between 50 percent and 85 percent of
the oxygen that we on the land breathe is produced by phytoplankton.
See Liz Cunningham, *Ocean Country: One Woman's Voyage from Peril
to Hope in Her Quest to Save the Seas* (Berkeley, CA: North Atlantic
Books, 2015), 64–67. See also NOAA, "How Much Oxygen Comes from

(as I write) to have killed already not one-third but one-half of the coral reefs supporting the life in the seas. "In the Caribbean, scientists had documented an 80% loss of hard coral over the last three decades."[7] And what of the dramatic rise in "red tides"— unusually harmful algal blooms now painting coastlines in Florida and Texas bloody apocalyptic?[8]

John's surreal nightmare narrates an oceanic catastrophe different from the biblical "flood last time." It shifted to "the fire next time."[9] His omen of the mountain thrown into the sea and filling it with blood is no nature documentary. But if you wish you can dreamread its crash in the great glaciers now melting and crashing into the Antarctic. Speaking literally, however, what does blood have to do with sea, besides saltiness? As Italo Calvino captures it in "Blood, Sea": our blood "has a chemical composition analogous to that of the sea of our origins, from which the first living cells and the first multicellular beings derived the oxygen and the other elements necessary to life."[10] John knew no chemistry. Yet in his hallucinatory oceanography, the blood merges toxically with the flames and with the sea, poisoning "one-third of the sea. . . ." Odd then to read that "ocean water has become *30 percent* more acidic—faster than any known change in ocean chemistry in the last 50 million years."[11] In the tiny stretch of the

the Ocean? At Least Half of Earth's Oxygen Comes from the Ocean," *National Ocean Service* (June 12, 2020).

7. Cunningham, *Ocean Country*, 43.

8. NOAA, "Gulf of Mexico/Florida: Harmful Algal Blooms," *National Ocean Service* (May 10, 2020).

9. Amidst the differential effects of global warming and pandemic fevers James Baldwin's prophetic exposure of racism echoes anew: *The Fire Next Time* (New York: Vintage, 1962).

10. Italo Calvino, *t zero*, trans. William Weaver (Orlando, FL: Harcourt, 1967), 39.

11. The Ocean Portal Team, "Ocean Acidification," *Smithsonian*

last two hundred years, "fire"—flaming in the furnaces of the fossil fuel industry—has indeed driven the acidification. About a quarter of the carbon dioxide released by burning coal, oil, and gas dissolves into the ocean. Scientists had hoped that by absorbing excess greenhouse gas from the atmosphere, the ocean would slow climate change. Far from it, they realized: this absorption is effecting a shift in the ocean's own chemistry, lowering its pH levels, turning it acidic and therefore deadly to most of "the living creatures in the sea."

The scenes of the Apocalypse arrive in the trumpet bursts of a waking nightmare. Any correlation with contemporary science remains (I will doggedly repeat) coincidence. But the coinciding won't quit. It gestures synchronistically in the reverb between ancient foreboding and scientific fact. A destructive pattern of global power already at work in John's time has undergone epochs of dramatic change. But it has not been laid to rest. On the contrary, it seems to be coming to its fiery head—at least as measured in the lethal degrees of global warming.

John's seventh seal breaks open a scene of environmental devastation more threatening of the human future than the four horsemen combined. But as we noted at the conclusion of the first chapter, the pestilence of the fourth horse must be read, then or now, as an *ecological*, not merely medical, crisis. Its percussive rhythm of hoofbeats accompanies the trumpet septet.[12]

Institution (April 2018) (italics mine). See also NOAA, "What Is Ocean Acidification," *National Ocean Service* (March 30, 2020).

12. Once delivered, the virus morphed into its lethal form for interhuman transmission. A leading ecosystems scientist, Richard Ostfield, says that "rodents and some bats thrive when we disrupt natural habitats. They are the most likely to promote transmissions [of pathogens]. The more we disturb the forests and habitats the more danger we are in." See John Vidal, "Destroyed Habitat Creates the Perfect

2. No Joke

The most yellowed cartoon on my refrigerator door depicts two wild-haired figures wearing matching placards, each announcing: THE END IS NEAR. One, the comic cliché of the robed street prophet, carries a Bible. The other, a nerdy looking scientist, holds

a book called *Climate Change.* The caption: "Religion and science finally agree."

The cartoon plays off the entrenched contradiction between science and religion. While that tension is as old as Galileo's house arrest and Giordano Bruno's execution, the placarded prophet is a spoof of U.S. Protestant fundamentalism. "The Fundamentals" were authored a century ago as a battle against liberal religion, secular education, and especially Darwinism.[13] Featuring a seven-

Conditions for Coronavirus to Emerge," *Scientific American: Ensia* (March 18, 2020). Vidal adds, "Only a decade or two ago it was widely thought that tropical forests and intact natural environments teeming with exotic wildlife threatened humans by harboring the viruses and pathogens that lead to new diseases in humans like Ebola, HIV and dengue. But a number of researchers today think that it is actually humanity's destruction of biodiversity that creates the conditions for new viruses and diseases like Covid-19 to arise—with profound health and economic impacts in rich and poor countries alike. In fact, a new discipline, planetary health, is emerging that focuses on the increasingly visible connections among the well-being of humans, other living things and entire ecosystems."

13. "The pamphlet collection of 90 tracts called 'The Fundamentals' (1910–1915) was backed by the Southern California oil tycoon Lyman Stewart, who hired A. C. Dixon, pastor of the Moody Church in

stage scheme of history called "dispensationalism," this version
of the Apocalypse awaits the imminent rapture of the faithful, to
be followed by the "Great Tribulations," in the fully plotted (and
ever-rescheduled) realization of "God's Plan" for the Endtimes.[14]
Starting with its anti-evolutionary fundamentals, the American
religious right comes well prepared to deny the science of planetary ecology.

What a joke—the opposites mirror each other in The End. All
too seriously, Revelation's own anticipation of climactic social and
planetary disaster does find an echo in climate science. As the
cartoon ages on my fridge, the opposite messages sync ever more.
Climate science has during this period shifted emphasis from
mitigation to adaptation—a polite way of saying that the Holo-
cene Earth, the world as we have known it for the ten thousand
years of so-called "civilization," can no longer be saved. Hope
melted in the meantime away from even the modest Paris Climate
Agreement to keep the average global temperature rise beneath
2 degrees centigrade. Then we learn that no, 1.5 is the limit for
avoiding catastrophe. We have recently reached the point of the
1 degree C rise above preindustrial temperatures, warmest in ten
thousand years. Hear the trumpets?

The relentless data of climate science does not, however, take
the cartoonish form of certainty in its predictions. To communicate the facts *as facts*, imbricated as they are in the uncertainty

---

Chicago, as general editor. Dixon put together a cast of conservative
Protestant scholars who then produced the essays over a period of
five or so years. The series exercised widespread theological influence.
For instance, Benjamin Warfield, professor of theology at Princeton,
wrote the essay on 'The Deity of Christ'" (historian J. Terry Todd, email
correspondence with author, August 13, 2020).

14. Matthew Avery Sutton, *American Apocalypse: A History of
Modern Evangelicalism* (Cambridge, MA: Belknap Press of Harvard
University Press, 2014).

of complex systems, has proven especially difficult in the United States. Here corporate forces and the Christian right wing maneuvered the margin of uncertainty into room for doubt. Exploiting the stereotype of scientific knowledge as certainty, the "merchants of doubt" deride as bad *science* the honesty of scientists refusing to predict exactly when, how, and how much climate change will happen.[15] (Recall Hamlet's quip about honesty as sign of doomsday.) In collusion with the anti-scientific certainties of fundamentalism, the way was prepared in the Reagan eighties—just as the cli-sci became irrefutable—for the trumping at the national level of every hard-won environmental policy.

It would ruin the cartoon to stick between the scientist and the fundamentalist a third figure: that of a religious eco-activist. She is motivated by both scientific and religious traditions. The eco-justice versions of religion build upon the scientifically informed Christian heritage that fundamentalism was born to fight. Such liberal/progressive theology features an evolving set of metaphors enmeshed in critical secular discourses.[16] It does not silence reflec-

---

15. Naomi Oreskes and Erik M. Conway, *Merchants of Doubt: How a Handful of Scientists Obscured the Truth on Issues from Tobacco Smoke to Global Warming* (New York: Bloomsbury Press, 2010).

16. The theological spectrum of the left presumes, particularly in process and ecological forms, a long-term dialogue with the natural sciences. Recent examples include Pope Francis's encyclical on climate change, *Laudato Si': On Care for Our Common Home* (2015); an anthology of multireligious and secular responses, John B. Cobb Jr. and Ignacio Castuera with Bill McKibben, *For Our Common Home: Process-Relational Responses to "Laudato Si'"* (Anoka, MN: Process Century Press, 2015); Clayton Crockett and Jeffrey W. Robbins, *Religion, Politics, and the Earth: The New Materialism* (New York: Palgrave Macmillan, 2012); Elizabeth Johnson, *Women, Earth, and Creator Spirit*, 1993 Madeleva Lecture in Spirituality (New York: Paulist Press, 1993); Thomas Jay Oor, ed., *Creation Made Free: Open Theology Engaging Science* (Eugene, OR: Pickwick Publications, 2009); Sally McFague, *A*

tion on the silence of God. It does not repress dire questions and doubts. Progressive theologies wear the mantle not of any preprogrammed and predictable apocalypse, but of the Hebrew heritage of the prophetic conditional: *if* we do not change our ways as a social order, our ways toward other humans and other species, then . . . the fire. And that "if" now demands attention, from all who seek justice for oppressed human publics, to the science of global warming.[17]

The kind of religion that opposes science on principle is what secularism—in its own dogmatic form—presumes to be religion itself.[18] So the certitude of a cartoonish religion mirrors and mocks the certitude of a cartoonish science: both cling to predictable facts. Caricatures of religion keep secularists ignorant of science-friendly forms of religion. And that ignorance only further diminishes the chance of a broad enough coalition—I sometimes call it *secularreligious*—on behalf of all earthlings.

Might the picture of street prophet and climate scientist protesting together hint at some new solidarity between spirituality and science? Sufficient masses of us can hit the pavement together to face down any doomsday certainty. Thus a tragicomic cli-sci docudrama titled *The Age of Stupid* concludes, after

---

New Climate for Theology (Minneapolis: Fortress Press, 2008). For other examples, see Further Reading at the end of this volume.

17. For examples of theology tying social to ecological justice, see Melanie L. Harris, *Ecowomanism: African American Women and Earth-Honoring Faiths* (Maryknoll, NY: Orbis Books, 2017); Michael S. Hogue, *American Immanence: Democracy for an Uncertain World* (New York: Columbia University Press, 2018); James W. Perkinson, *Political Theology for a Century of Water Wars: The Angel of the Jordan Meets the Trickster of Detroit* (New York: Palgrave Macmillan, 2019).

18. Richard Dawkins, *The God Delusion* (New York: Mariner Books, 2008).

"The End," with one more frame: "The End?"[19] All hail the mark of the question.

3. The Original Bittersweet

The trumpet septet of the seventh seal, however, is far from humorous—or finished. At the third blast, another elemental pollutant falls "on a third of the rivers and on the springs of water." "A third of the waters become wormwood, and many died from the water, because it was made bitter" (Rev. 8:11). Wormwood was the name of a very bitter-tasting plant used therapeutically in the ancient world, lethal in excess. In John's figuration the whole star named Wormwood has fallen into the fresh waters—definitely excessive.

What is carried in this symbol? John was not foreseeing the vast industrial toxification of drinking water, for example, how in Niger the extraction of oil by Shell has so poisoned the water that 150,000 children die there annually. These numbers feel abstract to us in the United States who, despite having safe drinking water from most faucets, buy oil-made plastic bottles, which then decompose into further poison. Yet twelve people died in Flint, Michigan, from lead-contaminated drinking water in a single year.[20] Or when the water company shut off water for four hundred economically stressed and racially marked families in Detroit—the city in which the poorest households face the "highest 'water burden' in the country."[21] (At the moment those numbers are being dwarfed by water shut-offs due to pandemic unemployment.)

John could not predict environmental classism and racism,

---

19. *The Age of Stupid*, directed by Fanny Armstrong (Spanner Films, 2009).

20. See Hogue, *American Immanence*, chap. 1, "American Exceptionalism and the Redeemer Symbolic," 22–53.

21. Sara Cwiek, "Report: Detroit's Poorest Households Face Highest

or our century's growing water crisis (though wars over access to clean water in the Near East would not have surprised him). He does seem to have been discerning a disturbing tendency for oppressive *inter*human systems to spoil the *extra*-human integrity of the planet. What if we say he was dreamreading a deep pattern—a history spiraling between the four horsemen and the seventh seal—toward ecological trauma? As one biblical scholar sums it up, "in Revelation, ecological disaster portrays broken relations between humans and with God." As to our passage, "In Rev. 8:7–12, there is a 'de-creation story' that reverses the creation story of Gen. 1.1–2.4a."[22] The leading American eco-activist Bill McKibben had years ago captured the human impact on our planet thus: "We are running Genesis backwards, de-creating."[23] Revelation's sevens—animal and brass horns, signs within seals— seem quite precisely to be reversing the seven symbolic days of Genesis.[24]

Not so fast, however. The trumpets persist, but they do not announce John's finale. Not nearly. Yet already with the fourth blast, a third of the sun and moon and stars darken. Then the imagery goes more phantasmagorically cosmic: another star has

---

'Water Burden' in the Country," *Michigan Radio: NPR* (October 26, 2018).

22. Harry O. Maier, "There's a New World Coming! Reading the Apocalypse in the Shadow of the Canadian Rockies," in *The Earth Story in the New Testament*, ed. Norman C. Habel and Vicky Balabanski (London: Sheffield Academic Press, 2002), 175.

23. Bill McKibben, *Eaarth: Making a Life on a Tough New Planet* (New York: Times Books, 2010), 25.

24. This reversal of the creation has a prophetic ancestor in Jeremiah, who is horrified by a vision of the earth, because of human stupidity and evil, returning to the pre-creation chaos, the *tohu wabohu* of Gen. 1:2; 4:22–23—"I looked on the earth, and lo, it was waste and void, and to the heavens, and they had no light."

fallen, and the fifth angel "was given the key to the shaft of the abyss." Bizarre scorpion-like creatures attack, causing unbearable pain while preventing the relief of death. I wanted to leave this to ancient monster lore but then was blasted into a double-take: the angel "opened the shaft of the abyss, and smoke went up from the shaft like smoke from a huge furnace, so that the sun and air were darkened by the smoke from the shaft."

The shaft of a giant furnace? What? Is John privy to the stinging future of the polluting industrialization that would fire up a millennium and a half later—the technology that would pierce the earth to extract its fuels and feed the flames of its huge furnaces? Surely he is not predicting the abysmal shafts of coal mines, the smoky skies blocking sun and poisoning air. As heard in chapter 1, it was "the working-class artisan, lithographer, and poet Blake above all others who saw the apocalypse coming in the dark satanic mills of industrial England."[25] His poetry, however, like prophecy, dreamreads *an insistent tendency*, not the futility of a foregone conclusion.

At the sixth blast, one-third of human beings are left dead. (It was on the "sixth day" that humans had been created.) The rest cling to their greed and their idols. John's story is not nearly over. It will get uglier.

So it is suiting that an angel now passes to him "the open scroll" saying, "Receive and devour it. It will be bitter to your stomach and sweet as honey in your mouth." Sweet to voice paranormal visitations, cosmic concerts, prophetic visions. Bitter, their bloody, burning, smoky contents. Gut feeling: not good.

---

25. Michael S. Northcott, *A Political Theology of Climate Change* (Grand Rapids, MI: Wm. B. Eerdmans, 2013). This British ecotheologian traces the current crisis to England as "the first 'modern' nation in the Christian West" (287).

4. Evil and Omnipotence

A dreamreading tuned to its prophetic ancestors discerns not fate but responsibility. This is theologically thorny. The horn players of doom are angels: *aggelloi*, "messengers." Of the rock God on the throne. Are we not forced to presume, along with most readers of Revelation, those who love it and those who hate it, that this whole fanfare of destruction is composed and conducted by the hard presence on the throne? But humans get blamed, while angels blast out the score.

So it is difficult not to read the scroll as it usually has been read: as wielding the force not just of pronouncement but of prediction; even of a prediction of the future based on a power to direct it. The deity seems not only to know in advance what will happen but to "permit" it—and so, at least indirectly, to will its happening (e.g., "its rider was permitted to take peace from the earth, so that people would slaughter one another . . . ," Rev. 6:2). Here we get trotted back into the classic theological problem of God, power and evil.[26] If God can foresee all these outcomes, indeed if they are expressly permitted, then why should humans be held responsible?

The angelic fanfare unseals the deep problem—the shaft of a theological abyss—of omnipotence. If the future is written in stone by the Stone, why on earth should we be blamed for the bad stuff? If it was all planned out in heaven—genocides, ecocides included—how could anything have gone differently?

---

26. David Ray Griffin offers the definitive twentieth-century statement of the process theological answer to the ancient conundrum of how a good and all-powerful God can permit evil. See David Ray Griffin, *God, Power, and Evil: A Process Theology* (Louisville, KY: Westminster John Knox Press, 2004). See also the wonderfully accessible Thomas Jay Oord, *God Can't: How to Believe in God and Love after Tragedy, Abuse, and Other Evils* (Grasmere, ID: SacraSage Press, 2019).

Where is the compassion in such control? In other words, how can an omnipotent God be in any meaningful sense *good*? Does "Good God" work better as a shocked expletive than as a characterization?

In Christian history there eventually came forth theologies of hardline all-control, most lucid in a Calvinism for which all that happens, happens according to God's will. We are predestined to salvation or damnation.[27] This sense of divine sovereignty degrades into modern fundamentalist determinism, which graphs out the seven "dispensations" of God's historical work in terms of end-time predictions. These get routinely and embarrassingly re-adjusted, but the notion of the precalculating God remains fixed. Always humans are blamed and punished, even while our deeds have been foreknown from all eternity. They are all, at least on principle, predictable. Neither double predestination nor controlling intervention resembles the visions of John. But certainly John's *pantokrator*, all-ruling, can be read or misread as all-controlling.

There is in the Bible no consistent sense of divine power as all-controlling. That is a later theological formalization.[28] There was among Jews, including those who followed Jesus, a presumption

---

27. John Calvin himself offers resources that counter the harsher Calvinist effects. For Calvin, love is the "capstone of the law" for humans and the divine. God can do none other than love—it is law—and God is not "a lawless god who is a law unto himself" (Calvin, *Inst.* 3.11.17). Calvin rejects "the fiction of 'absolute might'" (Calvin, *Inst.* 3.23.2). As theologian and activist Dhawn Martin insists, "It is rare in Calvin to find him discussing God's power without encompassing it in other divine attributes of wisdom, justice, goodness, faithfulness. God is not sovereign for sovereignty's sake. God is sovereign as love is to be governor of all our days . . . of all our actions. So, there you have it . . . God is love" (Dhawn Martin, email correspondence, August 14, 2020).

28. Beginning with the theologian Irenaeus, the explicit logic of an omnipotent God emerges. See my *On the Mystery: Discerning Divinity*

of One who calls forth the creation and encompasses its unfolding life. There have been endless struggles to hold the notion of divine power together with crises of unfair suffering. Much later this becomes the classic problem of "theodicy," of the "justification of God." How can a just God at once control the world and hold us responsible?

The breakthrough illuminations are not logical solutions but poetic epiphanies, like the voice in the whirlwind at the climax of the Book of Job. The voice is not claiming responsibility for any evils. It is celebrating in poetic detail the wild complexity of creaturely life—morning stars singing together, the "recesses of the deep," "the expanse of the earth," as "mountain goats give birth," the "wild ass runs free," the "ostrich's wings flap wildly," the "eagle mounts up and makes its nest on high. . . ."[29]

Yet Revelation, with its angelic and demonic agents of horror, does come closer than most biblical texts to an implicit predeterminism. This cannot be flapped away. On the contrary, we have in the United States and so the world to deal with its legacy of an apocalyptically charged right wing of Christianity that can read any disaster as a sign of the Lord's will. And if it is big enough, as a portent of his Second Coming. As a friend quotes his mom, a fundamentalist country farmer and denialist for years: "You were right about climate change, son. We can see it. But you don't have to worry. It means the Lord is coming again soon." I noted earlier that it was the closeness of the author of the *Late Great Planet Earth* with the presumed final president, Ronald Reagan

---

in Process (Minneapolis: Fortress Press, 2008). See especially chap. 4, "After Omnipotence: Power as Process."

29. From Job, chaps. 38 and 39. See my chapter on Job in Catherine Keller, *Face of the Deep: A Theology of Becoming* (New York: Routledge, 2003), chap. 7, "'Recesses of the Deep': Job's Cosmi-Cosmic Epiphany."

(long before Rick Perry proclaimed Trump "the chosen one"[30]), that provoked me to write a twentieth-century work on the Apocalypse. I was not worried that history would end by divinely planned thermonuclear exchange. I was concerned at what policies and politics could henceforth—democracy be damned—be justified in His Name.

While Revelation fuels such determinism, it also messages relentlessly that collective actions have collective consequences. It lacks any straight logic of divine control. Every glimpse or word of God gets diffracted—through the multiplicity of messengers, the facets of gems, the polymorphism of imagery. So in the playing out of our septet, there is no timeline presupposed, no claim that God has always foreseen, let alone wants or wills, these outcomes. It is for this reason that prophecy true to its tradition anticipates much but remains irreducible to factual prediction. Omnipotence and predestination are later doctrines projected onto from the ancient scroll.

The scroll itself remains oddly sealed in its dream-metaphors— even as it gets unsealed and resealed through the epochs of its effects.

5. The Eagle's Lament

The vision vibrates with sonic intensities. Hear the eagle's mournful call: "woe, woe, woe to the inhabitants of the earth, at the blasts of the other trumpets . . ." (Rev. 8:13). "Woe," which occurs frequently in Revelation, translates the Greek "*ouai*," a cry or sound used to express lamentation or mourning. *Ouai, ouai, ouai*—the

---

30. Roxanne Cooper, "'Trump's Base Is a Cult': Rick Perry Slammed after Saying Donald Trump Is 'The Chosen One' during Fox News Interview," *AlterNet* (November 25, 2019).

onomatopoeia conveys wails of sorrow. Indeed there is convincing linguistic argument for a better translation: "Alas, Earth!" or "Alas for Earth." "Alas," writes Barbara Rossing, "conveys a level of sympathy or concern for Earth that 'woe to' does not. 'Woe to' suggests that God stands over against Earth, pronouncing judgment or a curse onto Earth. This has been the predominant interpretation. . . ."[31] But the more accurate reading is one of acute mourning.

Cosmic griefwork voiced by an eagle: this suggests a very different affect at work in the visions than the hard thrust of vengeance. "If we translate *ouai* as 'Alas,'" argues Rossing, "God can be understood as sympathizing in mourning and lament over Earth's pain . . ."—that is, the pain of all earth dwellers. This divinity would evince a compassion more kin to the letter of another New Testament John: "God is love." Another kind of power, radically different from control—a power that empowers, invites, cares—is trying to come through. There is no reason to think that this John quite gets it. In the letter from Patmos, God does "permit," somehow sanction, "the plagues to bring about Earth's liberation from injustice."[32]

How would the torments help? The hope seems to be that the taste of disaster might serve as a wake-up call. This reminds one of how environmentalists have hoped that early waves of climate calamity might trigger collective responsibility, even among those most responsible for its causes. Hence the disappointment when (even now) they "did not repent" (Rev. 9:20ff.).

As we tune to the cries of *ouai*, recall that they are vocalized

---

31. Barbara Rossing, "Alas for Earth! Lament and Resistance in Revelation 12," in *The Earth Story in the New Testament*, ed. Norman C. Habel and Vicky Balabanski (New York: Sheffield Academic Press, 2002), 183. The Greek reads, "Alas, earth-dwellers" not "woe to us."

32. Ibid.

by "an eagle flying high overhead, calling with a loud voice. . . ." This figure, which can be related to the eagle-like fourth of the totemic quartet surrounding the throne, is read as speaking for God (who isn't speaking). The insistent divinanimality keeps us in the medium of dream. Certainly the spokes-eagle conveys a regal authority—even as it hints that God can better be decoded as crying out in mourning than as cursing in judgment. Perhaps, given the monotheist tension between divine power and divine goodness, God's grief can only be heard, be felt, through an animal. The speechless figure of our first sign, the lamb bloody from slaughter, suggests as much. We are called into a work of compassion—in the original sense of being moved, of suffering-with.

As later orthodoxies developed the doctrine of the all-controlling God, however, *He* hardened into immovable changelessness. According to the doctrine of the impassible God, compassion, because it is passion, could not affect, be attributed to "Him." He becomes the One who cannot be affected, the Unmoved Mover of Greek philosophy. God's stoniness takes on a harder meaning. Omnipotence and impassivity can soon work together in a classical rationality where control, of self and of subordinates, becomes the rule. That makes love the exception. The apocalyptic griefwork gets numbed. And with that inability to mourn is not the chance of repentance—*metanoia*, a "change of mind"—also repressed?

To dreamread the eagle's cry, however, means to hear its lament: "Alas, earth-dwellers." And to hear it *now*. If it had been widely minded; if our species, enough of us, felt sorrow for what our civilization was then, is now, destroying; if the eagle's national appropriation had brought with it such feeling for all earth-dwellers; if we had listened, we white folk, to the voices of those we treated as subhuman, with their animal totems. . . .

The bald eagle has, thanks to a half century of ecological effort, soared back from the brink of extinction. Does its metaforce call its citizens now to mind what can yet be saved? If so, it echoes Joanna Macy's decades' long mobilization of ecological mourning as "the work that reconnects." The possibility of that work remains shrouded in a long history of loss, clouded by a shortening future. *Ouai. Ouai. Ouai.*

6. Ecogrief

In a world of mortal beings it would seem that without some work of mourning, responsibility for that world cannot develop. The ability to respond depends upon our capacity to *feel* response. And responding in care or in well-being, in comfort or joy, depends upon the openness also to negative emotion, to our own grief and to that of others. ("Blessed are those who mourn, for they will be comforted" [Matt. 5:4].) Otherwise what is there but numbness interrupted by needy or greedy desire?

In an epoch of mass extinctions and global warming, there is now a formal mental health research category named "ecological grief": "Climate change is increasingly understood to impact mental health through multiple pathways of risk, including intense feelings of grief as people suffer climate-related losses to valued species, ecosystems and landscapes. Despite growing research interest, ecologically driven grief, or 'ecological grief,' remains an underdeveloped area of inquiry."[33] In the meantime the losses amplify, putting the very sense of human habitation—of being at home, of belonging in the world—in question.

As David Wallace-Wells puts it, "parts of the Earth will likely become close to uninhabitable, and other parts horrifically inhos-

---

33. Ashlee Cunsolo and Neville R. Ellis, "Ecological Grief as a Mental Health Response to Climate Change-Related Loss," *Nature Climate Change* 8 (April 2018): 275–81.

pitable, as soon as the end of this century." That is not a language of determinism. Its apocalyptic "likely" keeps doom conditional: *if* we do not take aggressive action now.... And such collective action, retooling political machinery and concluding carbon capitalism, will take more than gradual understanding and one-by-one response. The secular author of *The Uninhabitable Earth* notes all too cannily, "You'd think that a culture woven through with intimations of apocalypse would know how to receive news of environmental alarm. But instead we have responded to scientists channeling the planet's cries for mercy as though they were simply crying wolf." Will such numbness yield to grief—only when it is "we" who are crying for mercy? And so, "no matter how well-informed you are, you are surely not alarmed enough."[34] Or in the young voice triggering lament and action around the planet: "Time to panic."[35] It is such felt temporality, no simple "The End," but a planet-pressured series of deadlines that carries the spirit of the Apocalypse.

Yet not without reason we fear that attempts to sound the alarm, to break through the numbed layers of denial deliberate or habitual, may just provoke more resistance, more defensive numbing, more distraction.[36] But so does the opposite, the resort to mere facts or the mere denial of facts. *Ouai*. Our defenses symptomatize our planetary unwellness: our environ-*mental* illness.[37]

---

34. David Wallace-Wells, "The Uninhabitable Earth," *New York* (July 10, 2017), nymag.com. See also David Wallace-Wells, *The Uninhabitable Earth: Life after Warming* (New York: Tim Duggan Books, 2019).

35. Greta Thunberg, who needs no introduction. That I started the chapter with another Swede confronting mass death is mere coincidence. See "Teen Climate Activist Warns EU That It's Time to Panic," *Associated Press* (April 16, 2019).

36. Michael Shellenberger, *Apocalypse Never: Why Environmental Alarmism Hurts Us All* (New York: Harper, 2020).

37. Lisa Gasson writes that "truth, at least in popular discourse, is

Apocalyptic mindfulness will help us not to "get over" our grief, but to move out of isolating paralysis and into healing action. It attends respectfully to the difficult, shifting experience of fear, loss, hope, anger, and love. It tunes carefully to the therapeutic dynamics of grief: "Mourning," writes Thom van Dooren, "is about dwelling with a loss and so coming to appreciate what it means, how the world has changed, and how we must *ourselves* change and renew our relationships if we are to move forward from here."[38] Demonstrating that mourning is no merely human response, this multispecies ethnographer demonstrates that Hawaiian crows also grieve loss—of companions, of chicks. And even of dead trees. "In this context, mourning undoes any pretense toward exceptionalism, instead drawing us into an awareness of the multispecies continuities and connectivities that make life possible for everyone."[39]

John's mourning bird cries out in the multispecies voice of that possibility.

---

either whatever a person *feels* is true with no connection to facts, seen most often on the right; or truth is reduced to a fundamentalist version of the facts, manifest as a complex fact-checking apparatus on the left—facts that carry no awareness of power structures that seek to manifest as first principles, anchoring truths that fix white, straight, cisgendered, able-bodied men as the ideal citizen. A political truth economy must listen for the revelations of others: not for a Revelation, which would reaffix political truth to familiar nodes of power ... but rather for revelations, or encounters with others that present the possibility of a society, of a world, where diverse subjectivities flourish." See Lisa Gasson, "Feeling Truth: A Political Theology of Revelation," PhD diss., Drew University (Madison, NJ) 2020.

38. Thom van Dooren and Deborah Rose, "Dangerous Ideas in Zoology," *Thom van Dooren.*

39. Thom Van Dooren, *Flight Ways: Life and Loss at the Edge of Extinction* (New York: Columbia University Press, 2014), 126.

7. Though the Earth Should Change

After a few more unbearable rounds of planetary destruction, human and elemental, the seventh angel's trumpet blasts. There arises in response a hallelujah chorus of worship and thanks to the "Lord God Almighty," with two elders from the throne room singing judgment on the powers of the world: "the nations were wrathful, but your wrath came." There is no escaping the fury of this response to the political powers of the planet. The *ouai*, as traumatic abuse persists, turns into rage—as grief often does. In the metaforce of God's wrath, it out-rages the raging nations.

The divine anger does not simply target all wrongdoers, let alone all humans. It is precise in its aim: the time has come "to destroy those who destroy the earth" (Rev. 11:18). Justice singles out those who were already producing the uninhabitable earth. But the outrage is not simply on behalf of the human home. Our magnificent "terrarium-aquarium" remains the earth of all the fierce and vulnerable species, of the living, bleeding oceans, the streams, the unbottled waters, the forests, the lands. I see no escape from the anachronistic timeliness of this ancient rage. The warmth of compassion and the heat of anger rise together in the Apocalypse—and mount in prophetic proportion to the planetary scale of ecosocial injustice.

To target the destroyers for destruction—doesn't this just fuel a spiral of violence aggravated by sovereign righteousness? Yet *not* to name the economic users and the political abusers, that small percentage of the human population that systemically subjugates the rest of the inhabitants of the earth, is to bow down before planetary destruction. Thus the great Jewish thinker Walter Benjamin distinguished "divine violence" from "mythic violence." Mythic violence uses the law to protect systemic injustice. Benjamin died fleeing the mythic violence of Nazism. The divine violence, differently, is *resistance* to systemic violence. For Benjamin, that does not mean waiting for God to intervene; it means *human* enactment of divine outrage.[40] The just outrage has been recently and game-changingly mobilized in the massively *nonviolent* militancy of the Black Lives Matter uprising against the laws' protection of police violence. Recent matters. Ancient reverb.

Dreamreading the Apocalypse, we do not get ecosocial data. We may however *get* the archaic insistence upon the interconnections between our burning issues. So amidst immense human suffering, with millions suffering the fevers of pandemic, we feel also the heat of an inhuman anger. Its fiery rage burns through the chilling paralysis of every denialism. It rises in the wildfires and the warming ocean. Does systemic paralysis begin to thaw too late—as one grasps the matter of the melting? Of, for instance, the loss—possibly irreversible—of the "deep ice" of the arctic—of *95 percent of it?* With it the loss of the Arctic's reflective ability to bounce solar heat back into space? The end of its ability to limit the heating that causes its own melting? Call it a feedback loop, call it a vicious circle. Or as one leading climate scientist notes, "I would think of the summer ice disappearing as the true tipping point we've all been afraid of with climate change."[41]

---

40. Walter Benjamin, "Critique of Violence," in *Walter Benjamin: Selected Writings, Volume 1: 1913–1926,* ed. Marcus Bullock and Michael Jennings (Cambridge: Harvard University Press, 2004), 245.

41. "The reason Arctic ice is shrinking so fast, and why scientists are worried about it continuing, is one and the same. There is a well-known feedback loop in the Arctic, caused by the reflectivity of ice and the darkness of the ocean. When the Arctic Ocean is covered by lighter, white ice, it reflects more sunlight back to space. But when there is less ice, more heat gets absorbed by the darker ocean—warming the planet further. That warmer ocean then inhibits the growth of future ice, which is why the process feeds upon itself." See Chris Mooney, "The

Of course, such data may just advance the creeping nihilism, the despair and numbing that as surely as denialism freeze up our ability to respond. The tips into "too late" cannot be denied; they can only and rigorously be *limited*. It is too late to undo much damage already done by fossil fuels; too late also to undo the losses of slavery or of the Holocaust. But it is not too late to alter the outcomes—in ways that will make a difference that matters, that materializes, in the futures of those pasts. And so of all our "continuities and connectivities."

This chapter's sign of "earth burning" wants to end where the eagle's call, no longer a curse, can also bless. Here we drink deep of the celestial silence. Here an apocalyptic mindfulness might even—just *possibly*—pause the ominous feedback loops of animal extinctions and human plagues, of deteriorating democracies, atmospheres, waters, lands. This is a courage of the heart, *coeur*, that arises through grief shared and action initiated. In it we face, we do not surrender to, our fears.

> Therefore we will not fear, though the earth should
>   change,
> though the mountains shake in the heart of the sea;
> though its waters roar and foam,
> though the mountains tremble with its tumult. . . .
> Psalm 46:2–3

Arctic Ocean Has Lost 95 Percent of Its Oldest Ice—A Startling Sign of What's to Come," *Washington Post* (December 11, 2018).

3

Earth Pangs
Mother of Last Chances

*A great portent appeared in heaven: a woman clothed with
the sun, with the moon under her feet, and on her head a
crown of twelve stars. She was pregnant and was crying out
in birthpangs, in the agony of giving birth.*

—Revelation 12:1–2

1. *Two Red Mouths*

Portentous she is: no other figure in the Bible, God included,
comes wrapped in so much cosmic signage—stars, sun, moon
all at once. So her acute suffering seems all the more startling.
Narrating this contracted vision, John does not downplay the
screaming contractions of labor. To suffer not the worst pain you
can imagine, but a pain worse than can be imagined: "like there
was pain but no person behind the pain," a "desubjectification."

Thus was the birth process described to me by a friend who
had chosen her pregnancy (and natural birth) with fierce resolve.
The agony yielded one wildly lovable being, crawling about in
joy between the feet of both his moms as we spoke. Without
her verbalization the "great portent" of Rev. 12 might otherwise
have remained hooded for me in its heavenly halo. For all her

colorful appearances in innumerable folk Guadalupes and lawn Madonnas, this figure's cosmic labor, its desubjectifying pain, has remained veiled.

Indeed the apocalyptic birth narrative, even with its gasp of realistic agony, does not describe the subject of *any* literal birth—or historical nativity. Its galactic metaforce depersonalizes its content. If apocalypse offers a dis/closure in and through collective crisis—this scene enfleshes the opening as the agony of birth. The portent cries out for a third-millennium dreamreading. Through what struggle for justice, for healing, for survival do we try even now to deliver new life? Do we recognize the cosmic stakes?

But suddenly the dream, already agonizing, turns to nightmare.

> Then another portent appeared in heaven: a great red dragon, with seven heads and ten horns, and seven diadems on his heads. . . . His tail swept down a third of the stars of heaven and threw them to the earth. Then the dragon stood before the woman who was about to bear a child, so that he might devour her child as soon as it was born. (Rev. 12:3–4)

Picture a surrealist video montage of two blood-red mouths. The lips of a vulva opening in extreme but natural pain as the infant's head protrudes. Then another mouth opens before it, poised to eat the blood-slicked fruit of her womb. The dragon, red as the blood, is crowned, but not like her by stars. He is smashing stars to earth. In his majestically misogynist voracity, he has this cosmos-woman in the most vulnerable position imaginable.

Consider the dramatic movement of the metaphors: ancient childbearing (without anesthesia and with high risk) routinely took the subject to the point of desubjectification. But more often than not, agony would yield to new life. Isn't that how much creative labor—evolutionary, artistic, conceptual, political, spiritual—works? Rarely in safe, smooth steps of progress, often in unpredictable throbs and self-emptying convulsions, in different degrees of agonizing struggle. The pangs might become intense, the losses acute, even tragic. But we *bear* the pain in the interest of the new. It is not that suffering in itself delivers (a baby or a project, a people or a planet). It is rather that the delivery does not happen without it.

And yet sometimes another quality of struggle threatens: the mouth of the dragon. What accounts for that shift from the pain, the birth pangs, of becoming—to trauma in the face of, the *mouth of, evil*?

2. Dragon Mouth and Tree Monk

Images called up by the shift to trauma flutter by anachronistically. Consider folk already laboring to make life livable for themselves, their kids, their communities. Then suddenly, the shift: and they are confronting the dragon head of white supremacism. Or people already grieving over separation from family, from everything familiar, courageously breathe through the contractions of starting life in a new place: suddenly a crowned head of anti-immigration comes roaring, caging their children. Or already struggling populations are attacked by a dragon wearing a crown, a corona, of pandemic.

This shift in the quality of suffering may also manifest quietly, surrounded by beauty. Drafting this chapter, I find myself on a little island (not Patmos), visiting a long-time friend. She is practicing the art of permaculture, studying it as she goes, developing her garden, her "perennial food forest," while preserving wetland and grass pasture. She brings to it a tough farmgirl background. The organic abundance of the garden delights—and provides subsistence. Dozens of new young trees have been planted since my last visit, chosen for their potential longevity in this habitat. Keep-

William Blake, *The Great Red Dragon and the Woman Clothed with the Sun*, c. 1803–5; graphite, watercolor and ink. Collection of the Brooklyn Museum, New York.

ing them alive, fostering their sustaining interlinkage, involves extraordinary attention to pests, nutrients, moisture. She does this physical work year-round, by the grace of the one leg remaining to her and of close collaborations.

As I visit, the weather is lovely. But for the past three summers unprecedented drought had reigned. For much of each summer, therefore, she, so differently abled, had spent fourteen hot hours of most days dragging hoses around—mindful of the shortage of water in the well—to keep the baby trees alive and nursed. A new quality of struggle has entered. Something pressing beyond the natural and the unfortunate: a qualitative shift toward the unbearable. This crip ecotheologian recognizes it as climate change; the local climatologist says it is a "dry run" for what to expect in the future.

I spot the red dragon mouth: the warning sign of a systemic voracity. It breathes the furious power that the dragon, as we shall see, signified for John. Indeed the dragon, or Leviathan, had embodied systemic human evil for centuries. No, John was not foreseeing the planetary destructiveness of carbon capitalism. He was seeing a multiheaded, multipowered force of world-scaled destruction that he would read (and we will read in chap. 5) as the econo-politics of empire.

Like the baby of Apocalypse, most of my friend's saplings stay alive. She calls herself a "tree monk." The discipline is arduous, relentless, mindful. For now, ever facing the pressures of climate development and the vulnerability of these few regenerating acres, she is thwarting the dragon.

3. Writhing in Possibility

> What might have been and what has been
> Point to one end, which is always present.
> T.S. Eliot, "Burnt Norton"

As was the dragon thwarted in John's vision. However, far from growth rooted in maternal care, "her child was snatched away and taken to God and to his throne." A traumatic separation from mom and for her. But it saves his life. Who is this infant? "A male child, who is to rule all the nations with a rod of iron" (Rev. 12:5). That sounds as oppressive as the dragon power. A bit less so if translated accurately: " . . . who is *to shepherd* all the nations. . . ."

In the ancient imaginary, the neonate is getting identified as the messianic one who will liberate the world from oppression and keep it just. We watched him manifest cloudily in the first chapter, with sword-tongue protruding from head of white wool: another dangerous mouth. Yet it signifies the very opposite of the devouring dragon-mouth.

In the better poetry of Isaiah centuries before, "the shoot shall come out from the stump of Jesse / and a branch shall grow out of his roots." Something of a tree-monk, this prophet? "And the breath of YHWH shall rest on him, the spirit of wisdom and understanding . . ." (Isa. 11:2).[1] But also "he shall strike the earth with the rod of his mouth and with the breath of his lips he shall kill the wicked. . . ." That angry mouth attacks not the planet but its most ungrateful inhabitants. And there follows immediately the most renowned ancient flash of ecotopia, the renewed earth where "the wolf shall live with the lamb, the leopard shall lie down with the kid" (Isa. 11:6).

Along with such multispecies reconciliations, a fresh human beginning is imagined: "and a little child shall lead them." Indeed a baby signifies this new renewed planetary peace: "the nursing child shall play over the hole of the asp and the weaned child shall put its hand on the adder's den. They will not hurt or destroy on all my holy mountain: for the earth will be full of the knowledge of YHWH as the waters cover the sea . . ." (Isa. 11:8ff.).

Consider this reading of John's deeply Isaianic imaginary: the Jewish messiah, heir to the Davidic lineage, had long been expected.

---

1. Here I use the original tetragrammaton, the unspeakable YHWH, rather than the standard "Lord," in solidarity with its pronunciation as sheer breath. For a profound meditation on "YyyyHhhhWwwwHhhh" as the "interbreathing Spirit of Life," see Rabbi Arthur Ocean Waskow, *Dancing in God's Earthquake: The Coming Transformation of Religion* (Maryknoll, NY: Orbis Books, 2020).

He embodies the initiation of a messianic age. The revivified stump of Jesse branches into a great epoch of justice, mercy, gentleness—and ecological harmony. At last the radical old imperative is actually heeded: "you shall also love the foreigner, for you were foreigners in the land of Egypt" (Deut. 10:19). (In his White Pyramid, a late pharaoh snickers: take out the foreigners and the forests.) The hope has labored through millennia of traumatic trumping.

Most of Christianity has assumed that Revelation's child *is* "Jesus Christ." (Didn't you?) So the mother—she has to be Mary. Yet the apocalyptic birth scene bears no resemblance to the Gospel nativity narratives. And her cosmic signage marks her as anything but a human individual. The simplified Jesus-and-Mary identification distracts from the vision's collective scope. A more biblically plausible reading, made standard in the Reformation, was that she represents "the people," or Israel. Then the woman in her birth trauma summons up this poetic figuration: "we were with child, we writhed, but we gave birth only to wind" (Isa. 26:16ff.). Here Isaiah grieves a collectively lost possibility. He is calling his nation to take responsibility for failing its own ideals of justice, for yielding morally to the evils of empire.

And then so many centuries after Isaiah, just before John's time, the Romans have executed the one whom many Jews hoped was the messiah. John, writing about sixty years later, seems to be struggling with the agonizing question of why—so long after Jesus's transformative life—the messianic age was still failing to arrive. And the signs of the time signal to John that it is about to get worse. (Indeed the worst persecution of Christians by the empire began soon after his lifetime.) Yet in John's vision the baby is born living, though he is present for no more than a traumatic moment. Birth only to wind? Yes, but Isaiah uses the word *ruach*, "wind," which like *pneuma* in Greek, also means "breath" and "spirit." And breath and spirit also grieve.

So then why is the baby dude of the Apocalypse snatched up to the throne of the double gem? No warm breasts, those. We might dreamread thus: a possibility has come dramatically close to collective actualization. It was actually born, made flesh and blood. But systemic evil, with its sovereign horns and diadems, its power and wealth, arrive to nip it in the bud. John's dragon may have failed to kill the hope that Jesus had embodied. Yet the age of justice still failed to take hold. The failure is much greater than a single cross. After all, the empire crucified thousands of runaway slaves and Jewish rebels on those dead trunks. So the collective hope is tantalized, not fulfilled, by the experience of an individual resurrection.

Does the neonate being snatched and stored away mean something like this: the messianic transformation of the world remained, remains, *possible*? A possibility crystallized in dream, like the facets of a gem—precious but still lacking breath and life? Yet the messianic possibility would get actualized, some facet of it, in so many times, places, bodies, movements. But after the revolutions and the evolutions, hope would often fade. Sometimes swiftly and unbearably. Yet does the messianic potentiality, less abstract, more bodied than before, get somehow snatched, saved?

In the gemology of the unknowable, another world remains— not impossible. The prognosis two millennia ago was apocalyptic, that is, disclosive: it reveals the acute contrast between the actual and the possible. The contrast—between what has been and what might have been—makes the disappointments all the more agonizing: precisely because what might have been still has a chance?

4. She Who Flees

John's gaze does not linger on the fate of the neonate. Something else is happening: "the woman fled into the wilderness, where she has a place prepared by God, so that she can be nourished" for—a long time. This gynomorphic portent has come down to earth. She apparently needs its protective, nourishing ground. Desert retreats were a common practice of Jewish sages, prophets, radical communities. (John himself was on some kind of island retreat.) The woman's wilderness sanctuary divinely prepared and stocked for her could hardly be more hospitable. Under the traumatic circumstances, it seems to offer the perfect therapeutic environment, a place for grief, nurture, healing.

Who is this birthmother really? In context she may well incarnate "the people of God," understood as Israel and later the New Israel, struggling to give birth to the messianic age. But with her unique constellation of stars, sun, and moon, to pin her down to an allegory of the people or of the church seems limiting. With such cosmic attributes why can't she be called a goddess? The movement toward monotheism in Israel had shed all deities but the One as idols.[2] And in the patriarchal civilization of the ancient world, of course a One who becomes the Only would be male-identified. The singular YHWH could absorb the images and attributes of rival deities—thrones, swords, beards: *male* gods. And goddess imagery was usually and firmly suppressed. This portent, however, breaks through. Historians who relate "Rev. 12 to Greco-Roman sources often refer to the woman as the Queen of Heaven, who is surrounded by cosmic symbols in the manner of a goddess. Artemis and her Roman counterpart Diana were depicted with the moon and stars beside them or on the ornaments they wore. A moon goddess could be shown with stars encircling her head."[3]

---

2. On how the early Hebrews slowly relegated female gods/spirits to unimportant and "womanly" tasks, until the male gods, soon God, replace the paganish heritage of early Israel, see Tikva Frymer-Kensky, *In the Wake of the Goddesses: Women, Culture, and the Biblical Transformation of Pagan Myth* (New York: Free Press, 1992).

3. Craig R. Koester, *Revelation: A New Translation with Introduction*

The twelve stars evoke the constellations of the ancient zodiac.[4] She also has a likeness to the Egyptian goddess Isis, "the beautiful essence of all the gods," who in the prior couple of centuries, in Ptolemaic times, lent shape to the whole universe.[5] In her biblical forcefield she calls to mind the figure of Hochma, Wisdom, she who teaches us to walk with her "along the paths of justice," who "was set up . . . at the first, before the beginning of the earth" (Prov. 20:23).

Notice also that the Sunwoman's astronomical Gestalt occupies the vantage point of the earth. The crowning stars are above and beyond her head, her garment of sun cloaks her like the solar system, and the moon "underfoot" is the closest body, placed as it is beneath the earth while the sun is out. That does not make her a Gaia figure. A Mother Earth identity would account for the terrestrial perspective. But it would not capture the reach of her astronomy. Nor would it account for her revelatory relationship *to* the earth, *Ge,* as to another and perhaps subsequent character, who as it turns out will soon appear. . . .

5. Birth Trauma, Earth Trauma

Before Ge shows up, however, we are subjected to several verses of a war that "broke out in heaven; Michael and his angels fought against the dragon. The dragon and his angels fought back, but

---

and Commentary, Anchor Bible (New Haven: Yale University Press, 2014), 528.

4. Adele Yarbro Collins, *Cosmology and Eschatology in Jewish and Christian Apocalypticism* (Leiden: Brill, 1996), 108.

5. In Ptolemaic times, when she had a presence throughout the Roman Empire, Isis was said to have formed the cosmos "through what her heart conceived and her hands created." See Louis V. Žabkar, *Hymns to Isis in Her Temple at Philae* (Waltham, MA: Brandeis University Press, 1988), 52.

they were defeated." It is at this moment of cosmic battle that we
get the first full disclosure of the identity of the dragon: as "that
ancient serpent, who is called the Devil and Satan, the deceiver of
the whole world," "the accuser of our comrades . . . who accuses
them day and night before our God." (Rev. 12:10).

With this collation of names multiplying like his heads, he
barely existed before, scripturally speaking. There is almost no
"devil" in the First Testament; and the term *satan* in Hebrew
means generically the "accuser, adversary"—no personification of
universal evil.[6] But let us not get in out of our depths. In John's
Apocalypse, things get simpler: good and evil present as purely
opposed, independent forces. This is something like the ancient
Zoroastrian dualism that the young Augustine would embrace,
and later, after his conversion, reject, as making evil a mirror
opposite of God, and therefore an equal power. In Revelation,
with armies of light and dark, indeed angelic hosts, on both sides,
the power of evil is not quite such an equal, but close. It takes
immense cosmic war to defeat the great dragon. On this plane,
Revelation's performance of the warrior ethos of the empire it
opposes is unmistakable: Stephen Moore relentlessly reveals how
John's mockery of the empire turns into mimicry—and thus monstrosity.[7] So then every later crusade, every Christian war, could
be justified as an ultimate confrontation of good with evil.

---

6. The Hebrew "*ha-satan*," meaning "the accuser," is used in the
book of Job to signify something like YHWH's prosecuting attorney,
making bets with his boss about the outcomes. He resembles Revelation's
"accuser," but is no principle of universal evil. As to the dragon—it was
sometimes identified with the serpent of sin in the garden (Genesis 3),
who also, by the way, targets the woman. Isaiah tagged the dragon as the
terrifying sea-monster Leviathan. But the latter just as often suggests an
altogether different kind of creature, a delight to God, who "sports with
Leviathan" in the deep, as with a playful whale (Psalm 104).

7. Stephen D. Moore, "Mimicry and Monstrosity," chap. 2 in *Untold*

"A loud voice in heaven" now announces that the devil-dragon-deceiver has been defeated by the "salvation and the power and the kingdom of our God and the authority of his Messiah." Michael's angel-forces are joined by a great company of human martyrs, who "conquered him by the blood of the Lamb and by the word of their testimony, for they did not cling to life even in the face of death" (Rev. 12:11). The ambiguity of revelatory violence and its double-edged S/Word is nowhere more evident. For here the divine violence works as one with the militant *nonviolence* of the lamb, which takes violence upon itself rather than return it in kind.

In chapter 12 the victory has happened only in heaven—in the realm of yearned-for *possibility*. Did messianic hope get ahead of itself? Is John suffering internal conflict with the disappointed roar of his rage? Must we begin to diagnose in the text an internal tension lurching toward contradiction—even a *schizopocalypse*? And don't I hear in myself a dissonant counterpoint of compassionate hope for us all and raging denunciation of current world-trump?

In the meantime the dragon defeated in heaven, as though in *principle*, gets thrown down to earth. Here, in *reality*, he is about to make everything much worse. On earth, *not* as it is in heaven. Then, now. Our next chapter will unfold the global politics of the dragon. But here John captures the tension in a wrenching opposition of affect: "Rejoice then, you heavens / and those who dwell in them! / But woe to the earth and the sea, / for the devil has come down to you with great wrath . . ." (Rev. 12:12). Joy above, woe below. And so we pick up again the wail of the *ouai*—not curse, but lament. Directed again at earth and sea.

The messianic hope remains "in heaven," out of reach—while it is wholesale ecosocial destruction that "has come down" to us.

Tales from the Book of Revelation: Sex and Gender, Empire and Ecology (Atlanta: SBL Press, 2014).

I read here the cloudy future of an ancient civilizational destructiveness so devastatingly potent that it seems bound to play itself out in subsequent history. All honest hope resembles at moments the desubjectification of our opening birth scene: the odds can temporarily overwhelm personal care or creativity. But the messianic hope goes harder: it faces into the dragon's mouth. Into a pattern that roars open to the length of the earth and to the depth of the sea. Birthtrauma becomes earthtrauma.

Where did the Sunwoman go?

6. Her Wilderness Retreat

> So when the dragon saw that he had been thrown down
> to the earth, he pursued the woman who had given birth.
> (Rev. 12:13)

The narrative here slams down to earth with the dragon. Now he pursues the woman with full fury. Can she reach her wilderness retreat on time? *Ouai!* "But the woman was given the two wings of the great eagle, so that she could fly from the serpent into the wilderness, to her place where she is nourished for a time, and times. . . ."

She has sprouted the metaforce of eagle's wings. The image here reprises the ancient prototype of liberation movements, of *flight* from slavery to a new collective life: "how I bore you on eagle's wings, and brought you to myself" (Exod. 19:4). Does she incarnate a new exodus in John's time? Medieval Jewish mysticism relates how "an eagle stirs up and cares for its young."[8] The kabbalistic Targum identifies the eagle with the Shekinah: that aspect

---

8. See Catherine Keller, *Apocalypse Now and Then: A Feminist Guide to the End of the World* (Boston: Beacon Press, 1996; rprt. Minneapolis: Fortress Press, 2004), 71.

Ancient Egyptian Goddess Isis with bird wings.

of the divine said to accompany the people in their wanderings. As a grammatically feminine noun, from the Hebrew *shakan*, "to dwell," the Shekinah came to signify divine presence with the people amidst exodus or exile. Her spatiality embodies the poetics of a psalm—"YHWH, you have been our dwelling place in all generations . . ." (Ps. 90:1). The notion of divinity as our very place, that within which we live even as we are on the move, appears in the Pauline citation of a God "in whom we live and move and have our being." This dwelling in God would later be called panentheism: *all in God*. In that dynamism of immanence the Messiah/Christos becomes "all in all."[9]

9. See Acts 3:28 and Colossians 3:11. This interiority would much later be called panentheism *pan en theō* ("all in God").

Such indwelling echoes also the figure of Proverbs 8, who precedes the creation and is a "master worker" and partner of "daily delight" in its making: the female *Hochma, Sophia*, or Wisdom. But in the prophet Enoch: "Wisdom set forth to make her dwelling / Among the humans / And found no dwelling place / Wisdom returned to her places" (1 Enoch 42:1–3). In John's vision do we see her withdraw to "her places"? Her retreat is terrestrial yet uninhabited by humans. How would John's urban communities in the Greco-Roman late first century have read her? They would not, historians claim, have missed the resemblance to the Egyptian Isis, who in the widespread Greco-Roman revivals of her mysteries appears as a goddess—with the great wings of the eagle.

Cosmic mother, Shekinah-Presence, Sophia-Wisdom, Great Goddess. . . . She flies in the margins of vision. And in the face of sanctified patriarchies. No need now to replay the twentieth-century feminist retrievals of ancient goddesses, or of the Abrahamic God's female aspect (*His* Shekinah), or of God/dess, or of divine femininity. S/he/it/they dwell among the experiments in progressive spirituality and its prophetic, agonized births and passings. They resonate with indigenous, Mesopotamian, and Asian goddesses, with whole hidden histories of untranslatable divine sexes.[10] Indeed the secularreligious intersections of gender alternatives with liberation movements have not totally miscarried, even in the disappointing deferrals, even facing the red-faced rage of the male supremacist dragon.

---

10. See Zairong Xiang, *Queer Ancient Ways: A Decolonial Exploration* (Goleta, CA: punctum books, 2018) for a reading that engages closely the queer propensities of different ancient deities, from Mesopotamia to Mesoamerica, that, albeit having been often gendered female, have emphatically resisted that sole sexual identification, which, as Xiang argues, carries a form of modern/colonial monstrification.

John is not accompanying me in this sex/gender struggle. But dreamreading doesn't mean agreement. Not even among feminist scholars. For instance, Tina Pippin, who has written extensively on the Book of Revelation, argues that "John's first-century visions don't share anything in common with contemporary activism for equality and rights."[11] I agree, almost: nothing except the liberation legacy of Exodus, the classical prophetic demand for justice, and its influence upon all Western movements for economic, social, race, and gender justice. But I can hardly disagree with a complaint I helped lodge: the women John doesn't call "whore" or "Jezebel" come down to either the virgin/bride in the end, or the traumatized mother in the meantime. Pippin characterizes the latter thus: "the Woman Clothed with the Sun is a reproductive vessel who is exiled subsequent to giving birth."[12] Certainly she offers no ideal of emancipated femininity. Yet in the text no One is sentencing her to exile. God prepared her a place—a safe space in nature—where she could receive, not give, nurture. Another feminist biblical scholar puts it more boldly: "God co-groans and co-labors with us."[13]

The narrative gives one further glimpse of her, beyond her hetero-repro-messianic-mom function. Here is what happens, before she makes it to her retreat: "from his mouth the serpent poured water like a river after the woman, to sweep her away with the flood." Imagine a toxically polluted river bursting like vomit from his resentment. I have to admit that the evening before writ-

---

11. Tina Pippin, "The Joy of (Apocalyptic) Sex," in *Gender and Apocalyptic Desire,* ed. Brenda E. Brasher and Lee Quinby (New York: Routledge, 2014; originally published by Equinox in 2006), 67.

12. Ibid., 66.

13. Barbara Rossing, "Reimagining Eschatology: Toward Healing and Hope for a World at the Eschatos," in *Planetary Solidarity: Global Women's Voices on Christian Doctrine and Climate Justice,* ed. Grace Ji-Sun Kim and Hilda P. Koster (Minneapolis: Fortress Press, 2017), 330.

ing this I took a sip of The Dragon's Vengeance—*literally*. To my surprise (though I should get used to the synchronicities of dream-reading), wine with that name was offered me to taste at a neighborhood festival. Grape wine fermented with habanero chilis: I bought a bottle for its exegetical relevance, red dragon grinning sadistically on its label, and will never have another drop.

Fortunately the woman is not overtaken by the toxic effluvium. Hear why: "the Earth came to the help of the woman; she opened her mouth and swallowed the river that the dragon had poured from his mouth."[14] Another graphic mouth-to-mouth, this time in reverse —the dragon mouth opens first, and the earthmouth answers. And so a prophetic ecofeminism reads back, so far back: The earth herself, imagined as a female figure, comes to the rescue of the woman (Rev. 12:16).

Another impossibly distant analogy, from a further Asian wisdom tradition, springs to mind. The Buddha sitting under the bo tree reaches enlightenment, his right hand in the mudra of touching the earth. Mara the demon lord springs to attack him. It is the earth roaring "I am his witness" that rescues Siddhartha.[15] The demon and his army disappear instantly.

Here is the contextually correct precedent: this is "not the first time in the Bible that Gaia has 'opened her mouth' to counteract the deadly deception of self-serving power and mindless consumption that her adversary the 'ancient serpent' introduced in Gen 3:1 and that subsequently made Eden uninhabitable." Brigitte Kohl shows that the earth of Genesis had already taken the side of the weak and victimized: she had "opened her mouth" to take in

---

14. The Greek noun *ge*, "earth," the root of *geology*, takes the feminine pronoun. Gaia is a personification of *ge*.

15. John C. Huntington and Dina Bangdel, *The Circle of Bliss: Buddhist Meditational Art* (Los Angeles: Columbus Museum of Art and the Los Angeles County Museum of Art, 2003), 64.

the blood of Abel so that it could cry out "in protest against Cain's deceptive denial."[16] We might say that this Woman Clothed in the Sun personifies earth's connection to the whole creation: she is the wisdom of cosmic connectivity. So she shares the vulnerability of earthlings. She is not the earth herself, who appears as an allied agent. Only because of this female solidarity does the Sunwoman reach her wilderness sanctuary.

Pissed at her escape, the dragon roars off to take it out on "the rest of her children"—among whom John counts himself. We do not hear of her again in Revelation. Is she lingering still, our connection to the universe, somewhere in the remaining wilds? In the meantime, how much more blood and bile has earth swallowed, to save as many of "her children" as possible?

How much more can Gaia take? The last chapter dreamread the race/class toxins poisoning rivers, the global greed spewing carbon dioxide across the planet. There seem to be limits to how much dragon-vomit she can absorb.

7. Dancing Mother, Publick Friend

But when the heavenly Mother is revealed, and is sought unto as freely and confidingly as the Heavenly Father, then will woman find her proper sphere of action.[17]

But wait, it is not as though the Sunwoman just gives up and fades into the materialities of the ailing earth or the impersonal astronomy of the solar system. She disappears from John's narrative. But

---

16. Brigitte Kahl, "Gaia, Polis, and *Ekklēsia* at the Miletus Market Gate: An Eco-critical Reimagination of Revelation 12:16," in *The First Urban Churches I: Methodological Foundations*, ed. James R. Harrison and L. L. Welborn (Atlanta: SBL Press, 2015), 144.

17. Antoinette Doolittle, "Address of Antoinette Doolittle," March 14, 1872, *Shaker* 2 (June 1872): 42–43.

she reappears in some surprising times and places, not so long ago, not so far away.

Two of her most direct manifestations took place early in what would become the United States. One is an eighteenth-century immigrant collective of millenarians. They do not expect "the end of the world" but seek a new place, a new age. For this group of women and men, the new world must be free of male supremacism both divine and human: "As long as we have all male Gods in the heavens we shall have all male rulers on the earth." After several years of harassment and poverty their community began to flourish. They came to be called Shakers for their proto-rock ritual of intense, rhythmic, unpartnered dance. A vision had announced to Ann Lee that "she was received and acknowledged as the first Mother, or spiritual Parent in the line of the female." Having suffered multiple births followed by burials, Lee was done with literal motherhood. Refusing marriage as indelibly patriarchal, practicing celibacy (the only reliable birth control), the men and women under her leadership shook a new possibility into realization—a pacifist egalitarianism of both gender and economics. The experiment found its inspiration in none other than the mother of Apocalypse. For Ann Lee was understood to be the incarnation of the Heavenly Mother: as "the woman spoken of in Revelation . . . who was clothed with the sun."[18]

A kindred incarnation of the maternal metaforce happened simultaneously. Left motherless at twelve in a family of twelve children, a young Quaker was radicalized by the New Light revival of 1774, got expelled from her community, and fell critically ill. Here is the recorded part of the vision that came to Jemima Wilkinson

---

18. Ann Lee led a community of radical English Quakers who arrived in 1774. See Linda A. Mercadante, *Gender, Doctrine and God: The Shakers and Contemporary Theology* (Nashville, TN: Abingdon Press, 1990), 53.

in her near-death state: "The heavens were open'd and she saw two Archangels descending from the East ... they proclaimed saying Room, Room, Room, in the many Mansions of eternal glory for Thee and for everyone. ..."[19] Upon recovery, she believed "Jemima" had died and been reanimated as the Spirit. [Space, spirit, room for *pneuma*—breathing room for an astonishing new public freedom?]

In an unprecedented twist of Christology, Jemima Wilkinson gathered a community that would refer to their leader thus: as the "second coming of Christ in the guise of the apocryphal Woman in the Wilderness, the Woman Clothed with Sun." Wilkinson's new name was "the Universal Publick Friend." The Friend preached and wandered, leading a processional of followers on horseback, flamboyant on a saddle of blue velvet and white leather, wearing black male clericals punctuated with flowing colored scarves, infamous for loose black curls in a time when all women bound and covered their hair. A collective of two hundred, many educated, some married, some single, gathered around the Publick Friend's revelatory preaching. They planted their community near Seneca Lake, New York, held much property in common, and nurtured respectful trade relations with Native Americans.[20]

In this incarnation, the Sunwoman refused the pronouns "she"—or "he." "Friend" served as this one's pronoun of preference. ("They" might now suit.) Sharon Betcher captures the inception beautifully: "In the refraction of one moment, the Friend apocalyptically unveils the bindings of gender binaries." The Friend remained celibate, but did not prescribe celibacy for followers. But the Friend is less the prototype for feminists who

---

19. Keller, *Apocalypse: Now and Then*, 233–37. Jemima Wilkinson's inaugural vision thus brings home the spatiality of John 14:2: "In my house are many mansions" (meaning in Greek, "rooms").

20. Ibid., 235.

emancipate the oppressed side of the gender binary—than for the transgendered who transgress the hetero-binary itself. Unlike the contemporary Mother Ann Lee, "the Friend declined the mimetic linguistic possibilities in the antithetical underside of the binary division and instead paradoxically performed a seemingly non-categorical gender, a third sex."[21]

As I head with my congregation (including one delighted infant) to celebrate Pride, I imagine the Publick Friend's horseback processional joining the parade. The Friend expected that "the Spirit who gave all nature birth" would soon "chase the dragon from the earth." In the bits remaining of the Friend's preaching we hear an intersectional radicality: "Hath not God made of one mould and one blood all nations to dwell upon the face of the earth?" Their one blood repudiates the bloodlines of race and of class. In Betcher's beautiful reading, "in the visitation by the Publick Universal Friend the earth itself . . . became the grounding universal." It "negated that proprietary version of the 'law of nature' which authorized the rule of men over woman." Instead is announced "an embodied universal that, moving by the energy of friendship, tried to hold open room not only for women, but also the poor, the orphaned, the indigenous."[22] And by what name did Friend call the community formed to dwell in the upstate wilderness? By

---

21. Sharon V. Betcher, "'The Second Descent of the Spirit of Life from God': The Assumption of Jemima Wilkinson," in *Gender and Apocalyptic Desire*, ed. Brenda E. Brasher and Lee Quinby, *Journal of Millennial Studies* 2, no. 1 (Summer 1999): 72–85. "But precisely what apocryphal 'phantasm' did this Woman in the Wilderness expect to face down? Could it be, as Winstanley had put it, 'that Beast, kingly property'—that is, the private ownership of land against which he led the Leveller's resistance? Or as hinted at by Robert St John, the 'beast-like presumption of mastery'—at any and all levels?'" Ibid., 83ff.

22. Ibid.

none other than that of the figure who will manifest as the present book's seventh sign: New Jerusalem.

The tough labor of messianic possibility has happened sporadically; it has taken place here and there, now and then. Perhaps it now invites us—with the authority of the Apocalypse—"to make living room in the new millennium."[23] The multiheaded dragon of race/gender/sex/class/ability/nation/species lives too, vomiting varied supremacist biles. Within the United States, where such radical possibilities opened with visionary force so long ago: Has any dream-chance of a "universal publick" of friends miscarried?

Still the birth pangs, the earth pangs, do not seem to have ended. "We know that the whole creation has been groaning in labor pains . . ." (Rom. 8:20). What new people can yet be born, what struggles borne? Does that Mother, Wisdom, Shekinah, Spirit, Friend not still come, and come again? Will she, will they, clothe us in a wardrobe of sun, stars, and moon? Enfold us in queer new intimacies with earth?

And may we help each other to retreat when we must, to survive, to heal, to be nourished? The better to face our particular apocalypse?

---

23. Ibid.

4

Vintage Vengeance
Grapes Divine and Deadly

So the angel swung his sickle over the earth and gathered the vintage of the earth, and he threw it into the great wine press of the wrath of God.

—*Revelation 14:19*

Señor, señor, do you know where we're headin'?
Lincoln County Road or Armageddon?
—*Bob Dylan, "Señor (Tales of Yankee Power)"*

1. Beast Rising

Enraged at earth's rescue of the Sunwoman, "the dragon took his stand on the sand of the seashore." No picnic at the beach, this. It is on that elemental margin that we face our fourth sign: "I saw a beast rising out of the sea, having ten horns and seven heads; and on its horns were ten diadems...." So the beast duplicates the assemblage of heads, horns, and crowns we witnessed on the dragon, who now invests the beast with "power and authority." John's dragon-beast code targets the multinational power of the empire across sea and land. But have the heads and horns of super-power ceased to exercise their power and authority? Even through centuries of Christianization and then of modernization, has the multiheaded monstrosity been defeated? Or has the dragon-beast replication continued to diversify and multiply?

Speaking of Christianization: in John's horror show, the mirror-play of systemic evil gets creepier. One of the beast's heads "seemed to have received a death-blow, but its mortal wound had been healed." In other words this mortally wounded beast simulates not only his master. At the same time, with phantasmagoric precision, he mirrors the dragon's absolute opposite: the multi-horned Lamb who bears the "marks of slaughter" but lives. The beast must be read "as the demonic counterpart to the Lamb."[1] This is not the simplistic evil vs. good we are conditioned to expect. In John's waking nightmare the beast of superpower performs a sinister mimicry of the power of resurrection.

If the Lamb signifies the killed yet living hope for the messianic realization, it is for an anti-empire: it is for the transformation of our common life into what Jesus had called—mocking the political status quo—"the kingdom of God." Now, however, as though mocking that very mockery, the beast achieves global triumph. "In amazement the whole earth followed the beast." What is intuited here about the awesome resilience of sovereignty? Humanity is now mesmerized by the dragon and his representative—not just overpowered externally. We internalize that power, we desire it, we become part of it.

With "a mouth uttering haughty and blasphemous words" (those surrealist mouths keep manifesting) this beast gets worshiped in the place of heaven's wooly representative. John wants his readers to ask: Who is this beast that mimics and mocks the

---

1. Craig R. Koester, *Revelation: A New Translation with Introduction and Commentary*, Anchor Bible (New Haven: Yale University Press, 2014), 577.

crucified Messiah?[2] For it is under this sign that a carefully coded message reveals its target to "anyone who has an ear. . . ."

John's parody wields its own double-edged S/Word. It mocks the beast who mocks the Messiah who mocked beastly power. In Revelation's context that unnamed royal beast can only signify imperial Rome: the greatest political power the world had yet known. But over time does John's blade also twist back against its own visionary intention? How does the beast escape any conceivable intention of John of Patmos—into the Christianization of the imperial power and so into the imperialization of Christendom? No one has captured the tragic irony better than the philosopher Whitehead: "The brief Galilean vision of humility flickered throughout the ages, uncertainly. . . . But the deeper idolatry, of the fashioning of God in the image of the Egyptian, Persian, and Roman imperial rulers, was retained. The church gave unto God that which belonged exclusively to Caesar."[3]

The double-edge slices back. And forth: through one historic crisis after the next, through multiple and contradictory applications, the beastly assemblage of the Apocalypse remains relevant and revelatory across two millennia. Harvest after harvest, the grapes of wrath keep ripening. But the resilient voracity of superpower has not ceased to mouth off. Through monstrously many epochs, heads, politics, diadems. But neither have the voices of apocalyptic resistance been finally silenced. . . .

2. Postcolonial theorist Homi Bhabha captured a particular stance of resistance among the colonized as "mimicry and mockery" of the colonizer. See Homi K. Bhabha, *The Location of Culture* (New York: Routledge, 1994). As noted earlier, New Testament scholar Stephen Moore has read the Apocalypse through this postcolonial lens; see Stephen D. Moore, *Untold Tales from the Book of Revelation: Sex and Gender, Empire and Ecology* (Atlanta: SBL Press, 2014).

3. Alfred North Whitehead, *Process and Reality* (New York: Free Press, 1978), 342.

2. Iterations of 666

To complicate matters, the sign doubles yet again. If Beast A has risen from the sea, Beast B now rises out of the earth. It makes all of the earth's "inhabitants worship the first beast." This second beast is often identified as the "anti-Christ," though that word appears precisely never in the Book of Revelation.[4] American fundamentalism has long espied the beast(s) secretly at work in all manner of international organizations, such as the United Nations or the European Union. So the authors of *Trumpocalypse* celebrate "the countdown to Armageddon" as begun by a president facing down Beast B, whom they read as a global conspiracy operating through a sinister, universalizing blend of "Great Mass Deception."[5]

With the apparition of the second beast John's dream-code turns numerological, signaling that "this calls for wisdom" (Rev. 13:18). The reader is told to "calculate the number of the beast." And an infamous number it is. What calls itself "Christian prophecy" has produced innumerable identifications of the demonic 666. Sometimes the beastly manifestations are quite concrete (even asphalt): you may be relieved to hear that "U.S. Route 666 in New Mexico was changed to U.S. Route 491. A spokesperson for the state commented: 'The devil's out of here, and we say goodbye and good riddance.'"[6]

---

4. The term *antichristos* appears in the Bible only in the Epistles of 1 John and 2 John (John of Patmos, as noted earlier, was mistaken for the author of the Gospel of John and of the Epistles).

5. Paul McGuire and Troy Anderson, *Trumpocalypse: The End-Times President, a Battle against the Globalist Elite, and the Countdown to Armageddon* (New York: FaithWords, 2018).

6. Frances Flannery, "666 in Popular Culture," *Bible Odyssey*, bibleodyssey.org.

In John's own calculus, 666 comes down to commerce. Everyone in the empire, he writes, has "to be marked on the right hand or the forehead, so that no one can buy or sell who does not have the mark" of the beast-number. Even if we refrain from fundamentalist predictions of skin implants to replace money, it does seem that thousands in Sweden of all places have replaced their credit cards with microchip implants.[7] The "mark of the beast" might meaningfully dreamread as the global reach of financial power: Which of us does it not mark, now far more than in his time? When John is soliciting wisdom, he is addressing "both small and great, both rich and poor, both free and slave." He "pictures a situation in which those who receive the mark can buy and sell, while those who refuse it are excluded from the marketplace (13:17)."[8] In other words, few humans, whatever their status, are exempt from this politico-economic system. But no matter how anachronistically translatable into the current global marketplace, John's vision was addressing his own. The spiral of wealth and power itself—unlike its "late capitalist" or "neoliberal" or truly "global" economic forms—is hardly new. (Our next chapter will focus on the apocalyptic metaforce of economics, in the vintage of the "Whore of Babylon").

In John's context, Jews and Christians "experienced pressure to publicly identify with the emperor if they participated in trade organizations." All commerce circulated through those organizations. For John's communities there also arose crises around the huge livestock market in meat sacrificed to gods and then sold; around the "graven image" of the emperor on coins; around "making the sacrifices required by imperial authority" or else facing

7. Maddy Savage, "Thousands of Swedes Are Inserting Microchips under Their Skin," *NPR: All Things Considered* (October 22, 2018).

8. Koester, *Revelation*, 604.

economic exclusion, or worse. And as Koester explains, John is "using parody rather than simply describing a known practice."[9] The mutual entanglement of the political and economic systems encrypted by John as global only comes unveiled, *apokalypsis,* indeed stripped naked, under the subsequent sign of "the Great Whore."

Yet already John wants to make sure his readers *get* it. He hands his people therefore one further, crucial clue: the beast's 666 code "is the number of a person." So whatever or whomever his readers whenever want unveiled, John himself signals a particular personage.

Why the cryptic code? Why not cough up the "person's" name? Was repeating the name too distasteful (as when so many U.S. citizens used the number "45" instead of the name of the forty-fifth president)? More likely he does not want his letter, which is addressed to seven different, widely dispersed urban communities around the empire, to expose its readers (and its writer) to needless danger. So when John exhorts readers to "calculate" the second beast's name, he is directing them to use the ancient tool of encryption known as *gematria,* in which each letter in the Greek and Hebrew alphabets is encoded with a numerical value.[10] John's deployment of this code had political effects throughout history. In the early Medieval period, for instance, to designate Muhammad as the anti-Christ it was asserted that he died in the year 666. Actually he was born in 632.[11] But we will see that John's 666 does not so much foresee, as remember. Someone.

---

9. Ibid., 595.

10. Ibid., 596. Gematria provided a tool of encryption through much of Jewish and Christian history.

11. Kenneth M. Setton, *Western Hostility to Islam: And Prophecies of Turkish Doom* (Philadelphia: American Philosophical Society, 1992), 11.

3. Two Ancient Traumas

Beast A, the one from the sea, reads as Roman power itself. John links its seven heads to the seven hills of Rome, and to a sequence of Roman rulers. That beast from the sea, incarnation of the dragon, bodies forth the global superpower of his epoch. The armies of Rome had arrived *by the sea*. They made land, as had the Greeks before them, with the monstrous terror of invading fleets. This beast's "haughty and blasphemous" utterances, emitted from an organism part leopard, bear, and lion, with the ten diadems of his vassal kings, is coded in an ancient language of abomination. For Rome was not demanding mere obedience and taxes: the worship of the emperor as a god was now a matter of civic duty and loyalty. The idolized beast then "is John's parody of Rome."[12] But what of Beast B?

The current scholarly consensus is that 666 encrypts Beast B as *Nero Caesar*. We remember Nero, the emperor of Rome from 54 to 68 CE, for "fiddling while Rome burns." Nero would decode as the one who represents Beast A and who imposes its worship. But how does this historical allusion work? Supposedly the vision-matter is all "to come." And John is writing at least two decades *after* Nero's death.

Nero was said to have fled execution by committing suicide. "Nero had at first been popular among the Roman people, but stories of his arrogance and cruelty earned him the hatred of many other Romans, especially many senators. After enduring fourteen years of his rule, the senators ... declared the emperor a public enemy and sentenced him to be stripped naked, hung up with his head thrust into a huge wooden fork, and publicly beaten to death."[13]

---

12. Koester, *Revelations*, 579.

13. Elaine Pagels, *Revelations: Visions, Prophecy, and Politics in the Book of Revelation* (New York: Penguin, 2012), 32.

There were rumors that he survived—like the beast with the mortal wound? John seems to be delivering Nero as the undead persona, the symbolic representative, of the beastliness of superpower.

An apt choice. After a fire devastated Rome in 64 CE, rumors had spread that Nero was responsible (at best, fiddling). "To deflect criticism, Nero laid the blame on the Christian community. . . ."[14] The historian Tacitus offers a graphic account of Nero's retribution against the Roman followers of Jesus.

> [An] immense multitude was convicted, not so much of the crime of firing the city, as of hatred against mankind. Mockery of every sort was added to their deaths. Covered with the skins of beasts, they were torn by dogs and perished, or were nailed to crosses, or were doomed to the flames and burnt, to serve as a nightly illumination, when daylight expired . . . it was not, as it seemed, for the public good, but to glut one man's cruelty, that they were being destroyed.[15]

Tacitus exposes the sadistic humor at play in these gala performances. If John's own parody performs the mockery of a mockery, it is not because his readers were routinely subject to these threats. Nero's actions had been confined to Rome, and in Asia the persecution of Christians was sporadic. But this past refused to be silenced. The burning of Rome, and then of the scapegoats, happened within John's lifetime. Does a pit of historic trauma underlie John's vision, clouding, fueling, and intensifying it?

Messianism had a militant side in Judaism. Jewish communities were divided on how to live with the Babylonian, the Greek, then the Roman empires, how much to cooperate, compromise,

---

14. Koester, *Revelation*, 570.
15. Tacitus, *Annals*, 15.44, quoted from Koester, *Revelation*, 586.

or resist. The interfusion of daily transactions with pagan deities added spiritual insult to national injury. Jews were heir to the Exodus—the very prototype of collective liberation. They were known in Rome for their rebellious inclinations, which came to a head in the First Jewish War. That "Great Revolt" (66–73 CE) culminated in a retreat of Zealot forces to Jerusalem, followed by the Roman siege, the storming of the walls, and finally the torching of the Temple. Nero was two years dead, but had begun this wave of colonial retribution. Bear with this account by Josephus, a Jewish contemporary.[16]

> As the flames shot up, the Jews let out a shout of dismay that matched the tragedy; they flocked to the rescue, with no thought of sparing their lives or husbanding their strength; for the sacred structure that they had constantly guarded with such devotion was vanishing before their very eyes. . . . Most of the slain were peaceful citizens, weak and unarmed, and they were butchered where they were caught. The heap of corpses mounted higher and higher about the altar; a stream of blood flowed down the Temple's steps, and the bodies of those slain at the top slipped to the bottom.[17]

Now listen as Josephus captures an immense chorale of collective trauma, as the sonic horror roars into the red visuals of fire and blood.

---

16. Jewish scholar and historian Josephus (who had commanded a military unit at Galilee against the Romans), surrendered and became an interpreter.

17. Titus Flavius Josephus, *The Jewish War*, ed. Gaalya Cornfeld (Grand Rapids, MI: Zondervan, 1982).

There were the war cries of the Roman legions as they swept onwards . . . , the yells of the rebels encircled by fire and sword, the panic of the people who . . . fled into the arms of the enemy, and their shrieks as they met their fate. The cries on the hill blended with those of the multitudes in the city below; and now many people who were exhausted . . . as a result of hunger, when they beheld the Temple on fire, found strength once more to lament and wail. . . . The Temple Mount, everywhere enveloped in flames, seemed to be boiling over from its base; yet the blood seemed more abundant than the flames and the numbers of the slain greater than those of the slayers.[18]

It is hard not to read the destruction of the Second Temple as the specific trauma that the Jesus of Matthew's narrative laments a generation in advance, in his anticipation of the apocalyptic "birthpangs." He points at the structures of the temple and says, "You see all these, do you not? Truly I tell you, not one stone will be left here upon another; all will be thrown down." Then there will be "great suffering, such as has not been from the beginning of the world" (Matt. 24:1, 21).

We can therefore read these ancient communal traumas as forever encrypted in the Nero-number. Trauma, as it is now understood, is characterized by its strange temporality, the past-present of a torment that will not fully recede into the past, with flashbacks of a suffering that seems to be taking place *now*. The traumatic affect can at any time flame up again. In this way "Nero" has not died but "with the mortal wound" lives—in the systemic multiplication of oppressions, as the beast "deceives the inhabitants of the earth." And the deception hardly fades in calmer

---

18. Ibid.

times, when the shrieks of the victims fade into the background, into the normalcies of everyday consumption, the *pax romana* of imperial ongoingness. In its resilient, diverse forms, and across multiple current republics—its deceits are evident among those who can garishly exercise global dominance. But smaller states need not relinquish the imperial model. (Two liberation theologians in Brazil have been referring on Twitter to President Bolsonaro, he who presides over destruction of the trees and tribes of the Amazon, as "BolsoNero."[19])

4. Mourning and Justice

No wonder John's beastly parody is tinged with bitterness. If over a century later his scroll would seal the Christian Bible itself with gore, that was through no choice of his. He was writing a letter, not a canonical text. But it bears, as we saw with its Heavenly Mother, an unresolved trauma, a suffering demanding a justice it is not finding nor expecting to find in history as he knows it— the history of monstrous power. The renowned German theologian of hope Jürgen Moltmann wrote lately, beyond all youthful optimism, of the "apocalypse of the past" itself.[20] The past needs unsealing—revealing as relevant history—or else it keeps us sealed in its repetitions. So the judgment toward which Revelation drives is imagined as a scene where the unresolved agonies of the past will finally find a hearing; when perpetrators can no longer escape accountability.

John's sense of the past is permeated by the Book of Daniel (one of many pseudonymous Jewish apocalypses). Daniel is the figure of a young noble from Jerusalem captured by the Babylo-

---

19. Dean Dettloff, "Liberation Spirituality for a Global Pandemic," *The Bias Magazine* (May 17, 2020).

20. Jürgen Moltmann, *The Spirit of Hope: Theology for a World in Peril* (Louisville, KY: Westminster John Knox Press, 2019), 202–15.

nian regime and taken on as advisor—and dream interpreter—by King Nebuchadnezzar and then Darius the Great.[21] In the history of exegesis the empires get organized into four (usually Babylon, Medo-Persia, Greece, Rome) to fit the pattern of Daniel's four beasts (Dan. 2:31–48).

> I, Daniel, saw in my vision by night the four winds of heaven stirring up the great sea, and four great beasts came up out of the sea, different from one another. The first was like a lion and had eagle wings . . . and a human mind was given to it. . . . Another . . . looked like a bear . . . another appeared, like a leopard . . . a fourth beast . . . was different from all the beasts that precede it, and it had ten horns. (Dan. 7:2–7)

Daniel's quartet of beasts from the sea then morphs into John's trio of dragon, beast from sea, and beast from earth, with the same animal elements and ten horns (Rev. 1:2). For Daniel "another horn appeared . . . a little one . . . and a mouth speaking arrogantly" (Dan. 7:8). Daniel captures an agonizingly long history of multiple imperial colonizations. It carries in memory the meaning, not the data, of the suffering of the people of "the living God, enduring forever, whose kingdom shall never be destroyed . . . ," Dan 6:26). And John dreamreads this polybeastial history nightmarishly continuing in the excrescences of Rome. It was not miraculously solved by Meshiach Yeshua, who also foresaw and lamented its destructive ongoingness.

For the long biblical prophetic tradition, oppression was nonetheless, after all, going to stop. A flourishing earth-world always

---

21. Daniel's scroll was written centuries after that, along with the legendary sixth-century BCE performance in the lion's den, at around the time of the Greek Antiochus' rule—a rule that included the desecration of the Second Temple by the erection of the statue of Zeus in 167 BCE.

glints on the shifting horizon. But if we miss the symbolically condensed history of too much anguish, defeat, and collective trauma, we also miss the chance to grasp John's "hope draped in black."[22] To mind the Apocalypse, as chapter 2 insists, means to partake in a work of mourning. Only then can we hear the eagle's "woe woe woe" not as curse but as lament for earth's inhabitants. The lament for what was cut down—for what was and for what might have been, for what was snatched up into the impossible—carries with it memory of what went wrong.

So then, is it only by way of this mourning that a pathway opens toward the possibility of justice? For justice judges not in a legalistic void but in the light of what might have been. What happens when justice and mourning get divorced? One can appreciate the impatience: "Don't mourn, act!" some activists were insisting just after the 2016 election. A well-meaning and unwise imperative. If anger stifles grief, doesn't its motive-force soon get poisoned by repressed and festering emotion? Unmourned loss will lock into paralysis or leak into resentment. But *out*rage can also share mourning, even as it releases energy outward, beyond the stagnation of merely private grief. Such rage, even hatred, may fuel needed change. A character in a short story by China Miéville ponders the perplexity: "But think, and you have to hate, because if you couldn't hate you couldn't love, and you couldn't hope, and you couldn't despair correctly."[23]

---

22. Joseph R. Winters, *Hope Draped in Black: Race, Melancholy, and the Agony of Progress* (Durham, NC: Duke University Press, 2016).

23. From a short story by China Miéville, "Dusty Hat," *Salvage* (August 1, 2015). Miéville goes on: "Come on, now, this is a flat earth, and the problem is there's too much contempt in the world and not enough hate. Hate is not alright, someone said to me once. I can't bear hate. And that's not about piety, it's about living well. How can I not understand that? That made me think. Because I'm full of hate, brimming with

Is it when justice avoids the waters of mourning that its anger dissociates from its compassion—its love? Is this when rightful outrage might twist into self-righteous vengefulness? Is this when passion for justice degrades into vendetta, rife for manipulation: into the next crusade against the Muslim, pogrom against the Jew, wall against the immigrant, chokehold against the African American?

The force of vengeance is hard to miss in John's rage. All those who worshiped the Caesar-beast, who did not resist his branding, "will drink the wine of God's wrath, poured unmixed into the cup of his anger, and they will be tormented with fire and sulfur in the presence of the holy angels and in the presence of the Lamb. And the smoke of their torment goes up forever . . ." (Rev. 14:10ff.).

In minding the ancient background grief, might we do therapeutic griefwork for unresolved traumas—not just of John's collective but of our own? And so empower new strategies of resistance?

5. Like the Sound of Many Waters

In the bitter heart of John's vision, justice and vengeance bleed into each other—as they so readily do for humans before and after him, personally and collectively, in reaction or in revolt. The Gospel call to "love your enemies" remains as alien to this text as to the civilization it denounces. Nor does it teach the rigorous art of forgiveness. The Apocalypse is no Gospel. Yet John does not advocate for violence. "If you kill with the sword, with the sword

---

it. But think, and you have to hate, because if you couldn't hate you couldn't love, and you couldn't hope, and you couldn't despair correctly. Not because of some fetish for symmetry, but because what matters above all is the utter. What's hate but utterness, the unwordable with a bad inflection?"

you must be killed" (Rev. 13:10).[24] In a situation where even failure to "worship the beast" can lead to execution, John (no more than Jesus) is not encouraging armed uprising, which would be tantamount to mass suicide, as the first Jewish War made clear. Tragically for much revolutionary effort, desperate for a long-denied justice: the side of the beast is so much better at violence, well armed and prepped.[25]

The Apocalypse can be read as an aggressive teaching of nonviolent resistance. As such, it anticipates something like what feminist political philosopher Judith Butler calls "the force of nonviolence": "nonviolent forms of resistance [that] can and must be aggressively pursued." She links such needful aggression to what Walter Benjamin called "divine violence." "Divine" remains here an adjective, not referring to a personal deity, but signifying the critique, the unveiling, of the self-justification of violence by a power imposing its law and order. In this divine violence shades into a politics of nonviolence.[26] Similarly what Philip Ziegler calls

---

24. This is pretty much what Jesus tells Peter, who had drawn his sword to prevent his rabbi from arrest (Matt. 26:52).

25. See China Miéville, *October: The Story of the Russian Revolution* (Brooklyn, NY: Verso Books, 2017). Miéville shows that the success of the Bolsheviks in 1917 was due not just to the justice of their cause but to the mutiny from the czar's army of hundreds of thousands of armed and trained soldiers: a rare circumstance that allowed revolutionary violence the victory against that of its beasts, the czar, the aristocracy, and then quickly the bourgeoisie.

26. Judith Butler, "The Ethics and Politics of Nonviolence," chap. 3 in *The Force of Nonviolence: An Ethico-Politico Bind* (Brooklyn, NY: Verso Books, 2020). Butler reads "divine" in Benjamin as always adjectival, lacking a nominal "God." Divine violence may be read as the "critique of violence" (ibid., 128). See Walter Benjamin, "Critique of Violence," in *Walter Benjamin: Selected Writings, Volume 1: 1913–1926*, ed. Marcus Bullock and Michael Jennings (Cambridge, MA: Harvard University Press, 2004).

the "militant grace" of the Apocalypse refuses "the mark of the beast."[27] That means first of all exposure of the injustice of the system. John is calling for "endurance and faith." He wants to assure his people that even though the beastliness of power and wealth will get worse, it will not last. In the future past of the vision: "It was allowed to exercise authority for forty-two months" (Rev. 13:5). What a hopeful deadline.

Decrypting the schedule is not our problem: but the "it was allowed . . ." might be. It echoes the "permission" granted the four horsemen (chap. 1). "It was allowed to make war on the saints. . . ." By whom? The passive verb remains ambiguous. But John evinces a divine determinism uncharacteristic of most biblical writings. As we noted in the second chapter, his text struggles with the meaning of divine vis-à-vis imperial power. The Apocalypse is not generalizing about "omnipotence." Nor does it anticipate the clarity of Calvin's *decretum horribile*, the eternal predestination of each soul to heaven or to hell. But John does decode the vision-images by way of a certain providential determinism: "For God has put it into their hearts [the multiple nations of the empire] to carry out his purpose by agreeing to give their kingdom to the beast, until the words of God will be fulfilled" (Rev. 17:17). Unmistakable divine collusion.

Because John is confident in ultimate victory, he can call repeatedly for "endurance and faith." This victory will be wrought by wrath. Yet the violence will not be human. It will be brought about by something radically other than human force. It resembles the divine violence that in Benjamin's language counters "mythic violence," that is, such mythic and legal justifications of violence as are instantiated in Empire. Such divine violence—as "pure power over all life for the sake of the living"—seems nowhere better illus-

---

27. Philip G. Ziegler, *Militant Grace: The Apocalyptic Turn and the Future of Christian Theology* (Grand Rapids, MI: Baker Academic, 2018).

trated than in Revelation.[28] Judith Butler offers a helpful distinction: Benjamin's agent of divine violence is "not a vengeful God but a God who is seeking to destroy vengeance itself."[29] One could read much of the Bible's divine violence as just that: the violence that cannot be avoided if the destructive spiral of vengeance is itself to be destroyed.

In John divine violence comes in multiple waves of judgment; we will soon consider what is poured from the "seven bowls of the wrath of God" (Rev. 16:1). But let us steep a bit longer in the affective ferment of grief, anger, and justice. The extremity of the oppression that John looks in the face, its Nero-face, from the perspective of its victims, lends itself to an answering moral dualism. The opposition between the torments of the oppressed and the triumphs of the oppressor fuses with that between the saved (their names written in the Book of Life) and the unsalvageable. In apocalyptic literature—Jewish and Christian—the binary was taking on a historically quite unprecedented absoluteness of good versus evil. But the very extremity of the opposition seems to yield the ironic mirror play of two wraths, two vintages: of divine justice and of mythic vengeance.

Listen, again, to the cosmic music: "a voice from heaven like the sound of many waters and like the sound of loud thunder; the voice I heard was like the sound of harpists playing on their harps, and they sing a new song . . ." (Rev. 14:2–3). In its pulsing oceanic roar, with thundering tympani, John hears a chorus of 144,000 "virgins" in the throne room, strange voices merging

---

28. Benjamin, "Critique of Violence," 250.

29. Judith Butler, *Parting Ways: Jewishness and the Critique of Zionism* (New York: Columbia University Press, 2012), 96.

with the high-pitched enchantment of harps, delicate sounds collected into an incomprehensible chorale. "No one could learn that song" besides the uplifted virgins. I am hearing the boy sopranos in Mahler's *Symphony of a Thousand*. Or the great wordless choir of "Neptune, the Mystic" in *The Planets* by Holst, voicing an unspeakable immensity.

Does John's oneiric chorale somehow answer the requiems of horror—like that heard in Josephus as the unbearable collective shriek of terror and death? Does the sound of many waters—flowing and raging, vibrating into a universe of strings, thousands of lyres lyrical as voices—begin to soothe the flames of a collective trauma that cannot be individually resolved?[30]

The high-pitched voices remain here all-male falsetto. We encounter at this juncture the jarringly pure masculinity of John's vision. These truthful first fruits "have not defiled themselves with women, for they are virgins." So the purity of these men untouched by the filth of women begins to align itself with the emergent dualism of good vs. evil.[31] A normative ancient heterosexism is here morphing into a spiritual misogyny reinforced by abstinence. It would prove endlessly useful to the gender hierarchy of the future church, most evidently in the exclusion of women (however virginal) from ordination. Indeed in introductory addresses to the seven communities, John had derided a female church leader, "the woman called Jezebel," in sexually abusive terms (Rev. 2.20).

---

30. Lawrence Langer describes how Holocaust survivors find it impossible to incorporate/reincorporate the memory of the camp—which is anachronistic to "linear" time: collective trauma can only exist alongside the survivors in a space that can never become incorporated into the human person. See Lawrence L. Langer, *Holocaust Testimonies: The Ruins of Memory* (New Haven: Yale University Press, 1991).

31. Catherine Keller, "Ms. Calculating the Apocalypse," in *Gender and Apocalyptic Desire,* ed. Brenda E Brasher and Lee Quinby (New York: Routledge, 2014).

And yet. Something more is going on, something gendered between dream and interpretation. It turns out that the pivotal passage is not so clear. Here is the literal translation: "Now these who follow the Lamb wherever he goes are maidens (*parthenoi*). They were purchased from humankind as first fruit. . . ." Yet *parthenoi*, explains Koester, "refers to maidens, or young women of marriageable age, commonly with the sense of physical virginity."[32] So the gender configuration crowding around the cloudy white animal—who we recall morphed early from a humanoid with breasts—seems after all to be rather queerly high-pitched. Such phantasmagoric ambiguities do not solve the problem of the sexism of Revelation's good/evil binary. They do not express the author's intention. But they might keep us from merely demonizing this uber-influential, demon-charged text. And from deleting its holy rage for justice.

6. Tag of Shame

Judgment kicks in now, hard. A first allusion is made to "Babylon"—another code word for Rome: "Fallen, fallen is Babylon the Great!" She will manifest as our next chapter's sign. But the anticipatory taste betrays her distinctive flavor: "all nations drink of the wine of the wrath of her fornication." Mmm. But the global consumers of her full-bodied vintage are now forced to drink a far more bitter draught: "the wine of God's wrath, poured unmixed into the cup of his anger." (In antiquity wine was usually mixed with water.)

God's wrath targets a specific international public: "those who worship the beast and its image, and receive a mark on their foreheads or on their hands." We already encountered this mark as encrypting economic buy-in to the beastly superpower. Now a

---

32. Koester, *Revelation*, 610.

new manifestation appears: Beast B makes an image of Beast A for the population to worship. John underscores something particularly alarming about this image: "the image of the beast could even speak . . ." (Rev. 13:15). It can even have those who disobey it executed. Yet the biblical tradition has always derided mere images as lifelessly mute: "they have mouths but do not speak" (Ps. 135:16). In a primarily oral/auditory tradition this muteness has always exposed the mere image as idol.

An artificial image that speaks: Was George Orwell dream-reading this passage when he depicted Big Brother as a speaking image on television screens in every household, monitoring the lives of all citizens? Or do you think of the current screens chattering with the commercials driving our economy, shaping our image of the human? Or of the talking heads to which "Foxangelicals" offer unquestioning faith?[33] Or even—as I gaze at my screen during the pandemic—do its friendly speaking images prepare us for some AI dystopia, some lurking cyber-fascism?[34] John at any rate signals that the Nero-power does not merely impose itself from a top–down political outside. In this it dimly anticipates the Panopticon of Foucault, who insisted that Power in modernity does not primarily work from above: its omnipresent gaze gets internalized. It does not so much repress as *shape* our desire.[35]

---

33. Catherine Keller, "Foxangelicals, Political Theology, and Friends," in *Doing Theology in the Age of Trump: A Critical Report on Christian Nationalism*, ed. Jeffrey W. Robbins and Clayton Crockett (Eugene, OR: Cascade Books, 2018).

34. See Eric Trozzo, *The Cyberdimension: A Political Theology of Cyberspace and Cybersecurity* (Eugene, OR: Cascade Books, 2019).

35. Foucault's "panopticism" is derived from Jeremy Bentham's proposal of a model for a modern prison, the "Panopticon," with a watchtower at the center exposing all cells to constant view. Foucault analyzes how discipline produces individuals who act "on their own" to serve the interests of power. See Michel Foucault, "Panopticism," pt.

John's global idol of Power solicits the inward commitment, the desire, the thirst that this wine/sex-flavored "worship" signifies.

Now the humanoid on the white cloud appears again, responding to "loud" incitement from an angel: "Use your sickle and reap, for the hour to reap has come, because the harvest of the earth is fully ripe." The humanoid obliges, "and the earth was reaped." Thus are gathered "the clusters of the vine of the earth, for its grapes are ripe." The angel "gathered the vintage of the earth, and he threw it into the great wine press of the wrath of God." Here originates the metaforce of the grapes of wrath. "And the wine press was trodden ... and blood flowed from the wine press." Divine violence now flows to new heights: the blood-wine flows "as high as a horse's bridle, for a distance of about two hundred miles" (Rev. 14:19f.). Plenty for all who had bought into the beast to "drink." With hallucinatory precision, it parodies the "wine of the wrath of her fornication."

This bloody flood seems to carry the traumatic memory of Jewish and Christian blood shed by the original "666." Again the apocalyptic opposition of good and evil manifests as a mirror play, inverting the golden rule. God's wrath does unto the other what the other has done unto God's own. Both divine and imperial violence seem to make a mockery of the Eucharist, that ancient rite of wine drinking in remembrance of the life shared, the blood shed, by a nonviolent agitator. Here the messianic appears not as the lamb-victim of Rome but as the bloody victor. And the specters of centuries of Christian victimization of others—the wrong Christians, the non-Christians—fill the stadium.[36]

3, chap. 3, in *Discipline and Punish: The Birth of the Prison*, trans. Alan Sheridan (New York: Vintage Books, 1995, 1977).

36. In his *On the Genealogy of Morals*, Nietzsche quotes Tertullian to compare sports to Christian worship: "'[I]nstead of athletes we have our martyrs; we want blood, well then, we have the blood of Christ.'"

Yet there remains the other way of reading the battle: divine violence does not cancel a just nonviolence but makes it possible. At least this is the clear meaning in the Epistle to the Romans, written by a contemporary of John. "Do not repay anyone evil for evil. . . . If it is possible, so far as it depends on you, live peaceably with all." The nonviolent ethos is in Paul much more consistent—but similarly reinforced: "leave room for the wrath of God. For it is written, Vengeance is mine, says the Lord" (Rom. 12:19). John is leaving room indeed, hundreds of miles of it. He does not call his people to armed vengeance or revolt. But the textual effects bleed beyond any intention. After all, aren't we made in that Lord's image? Called to be his instrument?

His terrible swift sword?

That bloody cluster of grape and sword got pressed—again, with music—into modern political service: "Mine eyes have seen the glory of the coming of the Lord / He is trampling out the vintage where the grapes of wrath are stored. . . ." The poet Julia Ward Howe, an activist for the emancipation of slaves and for women's suffrage, composed the "Battle Hymn of the Republic" in support of the Northern cause in the Civil War. As Christ "died to make men holy, let us die to make men free." This war gives most of us who have protested more than one (beastly) U.S. war pause. However mixed its emancipationist motives, the Civil War did put an end to legal slavery. One can counterargue that nonviolent strategies could have eventually prevailed. Maybe. But how much later? Trample on, S/Word.

Back to the other hand: "the fateful lightning of His terrible swift sword" did not prevent the long decades of Jim Crow and of lynching; and then of persisting racism Northern as well as

---

See Friedrich Nietzsche, *On the Genealogy of Morals*, ed. Keith Ansell-Pearson, trans. Carol Diethe (New York: Oxford University Press, 2006), 30.

Southern; of the police violence provoking a second great wave of Black Lives Matter. Divine violence, however you sing it, has so far failed to defeat the beast-head of white supremacism.

Or of economic injustice. Now another iconic American literary allusion bursts in: *The Grapes of Wrath*. It opens with a full citation of the Hymn. Based on his prior work as a journalist, John Steinbeck's 1939 novel examines lives caught in the Dust Bowl during the Great Depression. These Oklahoma farmers were trapped in the spiral of drought, mass hunger, shifts toward corporate agribusiness, and bank foreclosures: environmental destruction and economic depredation operating hand in hand. Steinbeck's political intentions were undisguised: "I want to put a tag of shame on the greedy bastards who are responsible for this."[37] In a desperate exodus, his characters migrate to California (on Route 66). There they face unlivable wages based on surplus workers.

Hear Steinbeck harvest John's Apocalypse: "in the eyes of the hungry there is a growing wrath. In the souls of the people the grapes of wrath are filling and growing heavy, growing heavy for the vintage." The torment might dissipate in bitter acquiescence—or burst in revolutionary rage. Seeking a third way, the novel's protagonists struggle to form labor unions among the farm workers. For his hope that the unbearable ecosocial winepress of the Dust Bowl might yield a new solidarity, Steinbeck was widely lambasted as a communist. The novel does not depict an ultimate realization of its hope. It does offer an indispensable *apokalypsis*:

> This is the beginning—from "I" to "we." If you who own
> the things people must have could understand this, you
> might preserve yourself. If you could separate causes

---

37. Quoted in Melvyn Bragg, "John Steinbeck's Bitter Fruit," *The Guardian* (November 21, 2011).

from results, if you could know that Paine, Marx, Jefferson, Lenin were results, not causes, you might survive. But that you cannot know. For the quality of owning freezes you forever into "I," and cuts you off forever from the "we."[38]

This revelation of interrelation, this emphatic "we"—does it mark the movement from solitary grief into the work of shared mourning and collective transformation? In the liberation from the frozen subjectivation of "I" into the urgent assemblage of "we": even the idolaters of unrestrained capitalism get a chance to repent. A last chance? So also in John's letter: the call for change recurs. But "they did not repent of their deeds" (Rev. 16:11).

Does some aging, wine-pressed hope persist even in the United States? Though falling short of democratic socialism, the New Deal did cultivate new vines of solidarity; and those limited and embattled democratizations of the economy have not been totally lost. Nor have new waves of social democratic potentiality, calling for a Green New Deal, maybe even Dark Green, for an actually egalitarian democracy, for systems of cooperation in place of the beasts of repressive competition, been prevented.[39] Do *we* feel the vibrant, dissenting thirst?

7. Dragons of Another Deep

In the meantime the seven angels "go and pour out on the earth the seven bowls of the wrath of God" (Rev. 16:1). Again, the image

---

38. John Steinbeck, *The Grapes of Wrath* (New York: Penguin, 2006; orig., 1939), 152.

39. For the definitive yet engrossing history of Christian democratic socialism in Britain and Germany, see Gary Dorrien, *Social Democracy in the Making: Political and Religious Roots of European Socialism* (New Haven: Yale University Press, 2019).

confronts us with the accumulated consequences of our civilization—an *inevitability not of predetermination but of patterned
outcomes.* Nor need the fluid wrath signify a direct divine intervention, let alone vengeance against the planet. Indeed the angels
have just called for worship of the one "who made heaven and
earth, the sea and springs of water" (Rev. 14:7). It is after all the
very earth who saved the Sunwoman even as heaven saves her
child.

So now one of these bowls empties into the sea, which "became
like the blood of a corpse, and every living thing died" (Rev.
16:3). *All* of it now. Not just the one-third of the sea and its lives
we mourned under the seventh seal. Revelation's spiral of doom
stretches beyond even current red blooms and shifts of the ocean's
pH levels. So does the bloodying of the "rivers and the springs of
water." This bowl recalls the exodus from a much earlier empire,
when the Nile turned to blood—because the Pharaoh would not
"let my people go." Then comes scorching by the sun, "by the
fierce heat. . . ." Again, you might think Christian fundamentalists would take more advantage of such opportune coordination
of prophecy with climate change. We can however dreamread
John's letter as pressing grapes, blood, fire, red dragon into the
visible metaforce of an injustice that does finally toxify and over-
heat the globe.

I do not cease to suspect that the passages in John warning of
environmental doom—the relentless burning and bloodying—
have also functioned as self-fulfilling prophecy.[40] Given John's
position at The End of the Christian Bible and the mesmerism of

---

40. In my *Apocalypse Now and Then* I put forth this notion of
Revelation functioning as a self-fulfilling prophecy. See Catherine
Keller, *Apocalypse Now and Then: A Feminist Guide to the End of the
World* (Boston: Beacon, 1996; reprint, Minneapolis: Fortress Press,
2004).

his imaginary for two millennia, we cannot set aside the uses of Revelation to justify destructive politics and economics—the various Trumpocalypses of history. And the resultant earth-traumas need not but can be read as God's punitive doing.

Yet in this century I hear a counterargument just as strongly: Why blame one who cries out against the imperial injustice of global power and greed for the global effects of a carbon-drunk economy two millennia later? Why abandon him and his warnings of destruction to "the destroyers of the earth"?

So if John does have God *letting* the empire drink its own bile—how can this theology be read as other than omnipotent determinism? Perhaps this way: the hard rock God lets humanity taste the poison and recognize the imperial label as vile. After five bowls we read that the kingdom of the beast falls into darkness and pain. But its people "curse the God of heaven because of their pains and sores" and "they did not repent of their deeds" (Rev. 16:11). Speaking anachronistically: no matter how clearly the sovereign denialism is revealed for what it is (recently in catastrophic, anti-democratic failure regarding the coronavirus, let alone planetary health) its believers do not hold their bully-beast responsible. Nonetheless the chance of "repentance," of an improbable transformation to collective sanity, is offered at each turn of the doomsday spiral.[41]

What, we asked, does the red dragon behind the decoded Nero-beast portend? The force of power running amok? A meme-me-me that forges its own "we," unifying against a scapegoat (or scapelamb) population to produce a white or national identity.

---

41. "If collectively we are to free ourselves from our insane course of action and respond appropriately to the global crisis even at huge cost, then we must have a passionate concern for the Earth as a whole and for all its people." See John B. Cobb Jr., *Spiritual Bankruptcy: A Prophetic Call to Action* (Nashville, TN: Abingdon, 2010), 181.

Fused in their consuming "freedom," they worship an imperial pattern that, then or now, holds the globe in the talons of its political economy. With the sixth bowl the "foul spirits"—the energies of systemic evil emitted from the beastly mouths—gather the human rulers "at the place that in Hebrew is called Harmageddon" (Rev. 16:16). ("Do you know where we're headin'?") Then the seventh: "the great city" splitting, nations falling, planetary havoc—human and elemental. . . .

And in all this chaos well ordered in sevens, John was not seeing, let alone presetting, the future. He is reading a pattern in his present: a pattern with the many-headed systemic force to shape history as we know it. Even now.

Read in their context, the dragon and two beasts of the Apocalypse are anti-cosmic forces.[42] John faces the stakes with alarming clarity: he was visualizing, he was hearing, a pattern already monetized and marked, normalized and—bloody resilient. Preparing the way for a messianic take-down of the empire, he takes it down in parody.

To the tormented author I raise a glass of red wine. A vintage darker than blood, and deeper.

---

42. There are other ways, even biblical, of reading monsters of land or sea as figures of cosmic force. Tehomophobia, or fear of the deep (in the sense of the *tehom* of Gen. 1:2) is the key metaphor of my *Face of the Deep*, in which I investigate the long Christian presumption of the *creatio ex nihilo*, the unilateral creation from absolutely nothing. I offer instead the biblically and existentially resonant notion of a *creatio ex profundis*. In such a creation from the deep, there is another way of reading the watery chaos as creative potentiality. And the Leviathan can appear as playful pet of God (Ps. 104). See Catherine Keller, *Face of the Deep: A Theology of Becoming* (New York: Routledge, 2004).

5

Porn Queen of the Apocalypse
Global Economy Now and Then

Come, I will show you the judgment of the great whore who is seated on many waters, with whom the kings of the earth have committed fornication, and with the wine of whose fornication the inhabitants of the earth have become drunk.
—Revelation 17:1

1. A Ferment of Fornication

It is an angel inviting us into that scene spiked with international sex and power. We were earlier offered a sneak preview of this intoxicating figure. She was getting served the "wine-cup of the fury." Now we zoom in for a voyeuristic, oops I mean visionary, close-up of "a woman sitting on a scarlet beast." She is revealingly clothed in the luxury products of antiquity: "in purple and scarlet, adorned with gold and jewels and pearls." And she holds "in her hand a golden cup full of abominations and the impurities of her fornication."

A rich cupful. Indeed, as we soon see, the richest. The apocalyptic aroma of this wine fermented of global orgies will identify henceforth our fifth metaforce. A caption tattooed on her forehead announces "a name, a mystery: 'Babylon the Great, mother of whores.' . . ." With its titillating bouquet, the wine drips red with the blood of victims. For she is "drunk with the blood of the saints and the blood of the witnesses to Jesus."

Virginal John seems dumbstruck by such sex and violence. So the angel patiently explains to him the mystery of the woman riding the beast. As with 666, "a mind that has wisdom" is needed to decrypt the code. The beast's seven heads are now identified as "seven mountains" (wink wink: the seven hills of Rome.) Its ten horns signify the nations under "the authority of the beast," soon, as the angel reminds him, to be defeated in their war against the Lamb.

First, however, the pornographic violence explodes: the beast, which in his global multihorniness had been drunkenly fornicating with Babylon, turns on her in fury. The beastly sexuality of her ride seems to flip into a sadistic strip-show: the ten horns and the beast "will make her desolate and naked; they will devour her flesh and burn her up with fire" (Rev. 17:16). Slaughtered, cooked, eaten.

Now John is told straightforwardly, "the woman you saw is the great city that rules over the kings of the earth." We have seen that Revelation is preceded by a long prophetic tradition of decrying the cosmopolitan seat of empire as idolatrous, greedy power. Each new Babylon echoes the first global imperium, the legendary Babel. Her incineration recalls the burning of Rome under Nero during John's lifetime, but only as the prefiguration of a greater conflagration. The first and second beasts, however, had already been identified as Rome: its sovereignty and its Caesar.

So what distinguishes *this* body of Rome? Why do the others turn on "her"? Her symbolically charged sexuality, her empowered femininity? Indeed many scholars have exposed the text's misogynist rantings. We will not neglect this feminist reading tradition. But first I want to ask: In the context of John's multi-coded parody of Rome, what does her maligned sex signify? What is the specific political thrust of his polemic?

The waters on which she sits "are peoples and multitudes and nations and languages." The great city's seat of power is pretty much the world. Her insatiable debauchery embodies the flow of global power: as the very *polis*, "city," of politics. Thus she rides the beast. She turns him on. But he suddenly turns on her. Does the woman-eating violence signal how superpower contradicts itself? Devouring the very flesh, resources, labor it lives from? Does its order, sustained by lascivious aggression, finally collapse from within? But wouldn't conflict or betrayal within the empire be better signified by the "horns" or even the beasts turning on each other?

"She" must signify a different sort of power. In the previous chapter we read the sign of the beast as the body politic of empire, of political power for the sake of—more power. So what does her imperious urbanity add to that of the red dragon-two-beast-ten-horn assemblage? Let me suggest that it is only as we recognize the specific *goods* of her urban allure that the internal contradiction reveals its meaning. Only then does John's elaborate and sensory parody begin to synchronize (anachronistically of course) with a monster contradiction of our own time.

2. Cargo

The fall of Babylon gets played out in more graphic detail than any other vision-scene in the Book of Revelation. As the city collapses, becoming the ghostly "haunt of every foul spirit," she/it is plagued by "pestilence and mourning and famine." John may have in mind the plague not only of the Exodus story, but the one that hit Rome during his lifetime, killing ten thousand daily (79–80 CE). Perhaps he was also dreamreading a pestilential pattern, and so the coming Plague of Galen (165–186 CE), the pandemic that begins the end of the western Roman Empire. (Would that my imperious city were not mourning a crowning virus at this moment of writing.)

After the repeated refrain of "the wine of her fornication," "the maddening wine of her adulteries," that is, the international affairs that "all of the nations have drunk," we hear that "the merchants of the earth have grown rich from the power of her luxury." In a flash the story of her fall becomes theirs. It is the story of one who says "in her heart: I will never see grief." Why should opulent power yield to mourning? Great wealth can always procure substitutes, intoxications, and distractions from loss. John echoes Isaiah's taunt of a prior Babylon: you "who say in your heart, 'I am, and there is no one besides me; I shall not sit as a widow or know the loss of children'" (Isa. 47:8). The arrogance of power is here measured by its denial of mourning: it hears no eagle cry of *ouai, ouai, ouai.*

Now the dark irony of the Apocalypse answers the denial with a haunting performance of urban silence:

> And the sound of harpists and minstrels and
>   of flautists and trumpeters
> Will be heard in you no more;
> And an artisan of any trade
> Will be found in you no more. . . .
> And the voice of bridegroom and bride
> will be heard in you no more. (Rev. 18:22–23)

The poetics of chapter 18 belongs to what scholars of antiquity call the "city lament genre." In another example much older than Revelation—the Mesopotamian "Lamentation over the Destruction of Ur"—we hear, "Woe is me, my city which no longer exists— I am not its queen; O Nanna, Ur which no longer exists—I am not its mistress . . . bitterly I weep." Barbara Rossing thus reads Revelation 18 as "a satirical city lament against Babylon, taunting the hated [Roman] empire with dirges in advance of its destruction."[1]

Yet the apocalyptic lament exceeds vengefulness even as it mocks Babylon's refusal of grief. Its poetry conveys a call that precedes the collapse: "come out of her, my people." That call to "come out of her" clearly carries John's concern that some Christian communities were too well integrated into Roman culture. But precisely what form of intercourse is here signaled? John's focus here is not the idolatry of Roman emperor worship nor the violence of beastly power. At the very conclusion of the elegy for the life-sustaining activities that are "no more," we read: "for your merchants were the magnates of the earth, and all nations were deceived by your sorcery."

Reading the text in the last millennium, I took the denunciation of these multinational merchant lords as mere moralism. I skimmed impatiently a related passage. It felt like an archaic inventory list, obsessively detailed, clumsy amidst the grandiose dualism of good vs. evil, of God-angels-messiah vs. beasts-demons-whore. Now I see what I missed. Read (and count) for yourself the full cargo list:

> And the merchants of the earth weep and mourn for her, since no one buys their cargo any more, cargo of gold, silver, jewels and pearls, fine linen, purple, silk and scarlet, all kinds of scented wood, all articles of ivory, all articles of costly wood, bronze, iron, and marble, cinnamon, spice, incense, myrrh, frankincense, wine, olive oil, choice flour and wheat, cattle and sheep, horses and chariots—and human bodies and souls. (Rev. 18:11–13)

---

1. Barbara Rossing, *The Choice between Two Cities: Whore, Bride, and Empire in the Apocalypse* (Harrisburg, PA: Trinity Press International, 1999), 102ff., 110.

Twenty-eight items: an inordinate amount of *stuff*, in a text of tightly packed symbolism. The cargo finally landed for me. The *import* of these imports: the vision inventories the luxury products of ancient Roman trade, conveyed over routes of land and sea maintained and policed by the empire. John's satire of the merchants' lament at the loss of their lascivious wealth bites deep: it delivers a loaded critique of what we now term "the global economy."

Roman writers such as Pliny the Elder, Tacitus, and Petronius list many of the same goods as examples of extravagance, Rossing notes. But "Revelation shares these moralists' polemic against decadence but goes much further, condemning the entire exploitative system that enriched an urban elite at the expense of the majority of the population."[2] Boozy Babylon, the imperial city, embodies the sovereign voracity of the global economy.

3. "Come Out of Her"

It is no accident that slavery, a commodity taken for granted by the urbane Roman writers, designates the ultimate freight on John's list. Rome two thousand years ago operated the largest market in chattel slaves on the planet. The trade was centered in the forum, where newly imported slaves could always be seen standing, feet chalked white, amidst shouting auctioneers. John is writing to communities situated in urban centers of the imperial slave trade, where human trafficking was business as usual.[3] A slave trader was a "merchant of bodies" (*somatemporos*). People are bought and sold as captive bodies. They exemplify what the political philosopher

---

2. Ibid., 8.

3. See Craig R. Koester, *Revelation: A New Translation with Introduction and Commentary*, Anchor Bible (New Haven: Yale University Press, 2014), 706.

Giorgio Agamben calls "bare life": humans stripped of any rights or protections.[4] To denormalize this commonplace John ends his list with the paraphrase of "slaves" as "human bodies and souls."[5]

The fact that chattel slavery would continue to reinvent itself in *Christian* form until the mid-nineteenth century, with its modern market source in Africa since the fifteenth, bears bodily witness to the elongated future of this text. The fact that "civi-lization" (from *civitas*, city) as we know it is based upon the labor of unthinkable numbers of slaves defines one historical vector of apocalyptic mindfulness. That three times more people are enslaved today than during the centuries of transatlantic slavery—over forty million, mostly women—remains largely unthought.[6] And then of course there are the billions who work for little more than slave wages.

With the emphasis on merchants and their merchandise, human and otherwise, John has added something new to ancient social ethics: "In employing the genre of satirical city lament against Babylon/Rome, Revelation 18 does not strictly follow the biblical or classical pattern. Modifications of the typical pattern

---

4. Giorgio Agamben, *Homo Sacer: Sovereign Power and Bare Life* (Stanford, CA: Stanford University Press, 1998).

5. Koester, *Revelation*, 706.

6. "The word 'slavery' conjures up images of shackles and transatlantic ships—depictions that seem relegated firmly to the past. But more people are enslaved today than at any other time in history. Experts have calculated that roughly 13 million people were captured and sold as slaves between the 15th and 19th centuries; today, an estimated 40.3 million people—more than three times the figure during the transatlantic slave trade—are living in some form of modern slavery, according to the latest figures published by the UN's International Labour Organization (ILO) and the Walk Free Foundation. Women and girls comprise 71% of all modern slavery victims. Children make up 25% and account for 10 million of all the slaves worldwide." Kate Hodal, "One in 200 People Is a Slave. Why?" *The Guardian* (February 25, 2019).

include the focus on Babylon's 'merchants' as the object of critique. . . ."[7] Ezekiel comes the closest to anticipating John's condemnation of global economics. Here the former addresses the maritime empire of Tyre: "When your wares came from the seas, you satisfied many peoples; with your abundant wealth and merchandise you enriched the kings of the earth" (Ezek. 27:32f.). The kings and mariners then wail at Tyre's destruction (in 332 BCE, by Alexander).[8] Yet John dramatically adds "a third lament, that of the merchants. This lament of the merchants becomes the structural center of Revelation 18."[9]

> Alas, alas, the great city,
> Where all who had ships at sea
> Grew rich by her wealth!
> For in one hour she has been laid waste. (Rev. 18:19)

In other words it is not only the fleets of invading armies that came by sea but the endless waves of cargo ships. John is satirizing not only the injustice of Roman trade, but its economic globalism. The double-edged S/Word reveals a cosmopolitan economy at once manifesting its own systemic dominance and parasitically riding the multinational beast-power. In an epoch long preceding the discourse of economic systems, he grasps after a systemic critique, beyond mere denunciation of the vice of greed.

To lambaste the imperial excess of power, violence, and greed, to capture in particular its economy of insatiability—brutally destructive and inevitably self-destructive—John has dreamt the body of a woman. If his people are called to "come out of her," the sexual metaphors remain graphic: pull out of the body of global

---

7. Rossing, *The Choice*, 113.
8. The prophet foretells the destruction of Tyre in Ezekiel 26.
9. Ibid.

trade; cease commercial intercourse with her. John recognizes the difficulty of withdrawal from this totalizing system. Not only does it provide needed jobs and goods, but at once gratifies and feeds an insatiable desire. John's mocking material specificity decrypts the economic system—viewed as though in retrospect—in its addictiveness:

> The fruit for which your soul longed
>> has gone from you,
> and all your dainties and your splendor
>> are lost to you,
>>> never to be found again! (Rev. 18:14)

This "soul" longs for commodities, while other "souls" are being sold *as* commodities. Power does not merely thwart desire or reward it—it *produces* it. In John's metaforce: power *seduces*. The Babylon economy reads out here as so internalized by its subjects as to keep them at the same time its objects. If slaves are the manifest symptom of human commodification, the merchants, shipmasters, and consumers of the global economy are bought even as they buy. So the graphic of the Great Whore signifies a commodification of self, body and soul, on the part of imperial subjects—not just of their objects. Our global economic system has been dubbed "neo-imperial" for half a century. Its product advertising runs slick with pornographic imagery.[10] Sexuality itself continues to sell. And to get sold. Particularly still female-identified sexuality.

John's Apocalypse, in all of this, operates "in accordance with an implacable cultural script that reflexively codes excess as

---

10. For the first articulation of neo-imperialism, or neocolonialism, see Jean-Paul Sartre, *Colonialism and Neocolonialism*, trans. Azzedine Haddour, Steve Brewer, and Terry McWilliams (New York: Routledge, 2001, 1964). Sartre wrote as formal European colonialism was ending.

feminine."[11] The very excess of John's vision of the whore, a slow close-up within the sweep of apocalyptic signs, taps the misogyny of his time. It mirrors ancient commodifications of sexuality in order to expose commodification itself. So I cannot repress the question any longer, it is growing rude: however noble, indeed prophetic, is his economic critique—is this John (upper or lower case) not serving up the sensationally fleshy ferment that he excoriates? Has prophecy become pornography?

4. Revealing Pornē-graphy

John's graphic is literally pornographic. Or rather (to the letter) pornēgraphic. The term that John writes as Babylon's title is *pornē*. This Greek word for prostitute is to be distinguished from the term we might have expected for a dazzlingly adorned icon of Roman luxury: *hetaira*, "courtesan." "Recognition of the difference between a pornē and a courtesan is essential for appreciating the bite of ancient Roman invective." The hetaira from the late fourth century BCE was a "recognizable type in Athenian comic drama in particular," sometimes celebrated for her wit and consorting with illustrious men. She was, Stephen Moore explains, "by definition an unmarriageable woman not under the control of a father, husband or pimp," who made her way in the world "by sexually attracting propertied men." She had dignity of name and public presence. In stark contrast, the *pornē* "belonged to the streets: she was the hetaira's nameless, faceless brothel counterpart, and participated in a type of commodity exchange that continually depersonified and reified."[12]

---

11. Stephen D. Moore, *Untold Tales from the Book of Revelation: Sex and Gender, Empire and Ecology* (Atlanta: SBL Press, 2014), 119.

12. Laura K. McClure, *Courtesans at Table: Gender and Greek Literary Culture in Athenaeus* (New York: Routledge, 2003), 18.

In other words the *pornē* of Revelation 17 is to be regarded "as a whore of the most degraded kind, a tattooed slave."[13] "Unlike a hetaira loyal to a single man, Babylon is spectacularly promiscuous, servicing all the kings of the earth. With her name emblazoned on her forehead, she is implicitly marked as a slave, thereby sharing the status of so many flesh-and-blood brothel workers of the empire. Yet at the same time, Babylon calls herself a queen/empress."[14] So in Moore's exegesis, "Revelation 17–18 presents us with "the paradox of *an enthroned pornē*. . . ."[15] This tensive symbol of total commodification—into the depths of one's own flesh—signifies at once enslavement and its opposite, sovereign rule.

John's satire of the political economy of Rome is performed by that paradox. In the hypermasculinism of the empire and its warrior-rulers, no image—not even of beastly monsters—could be more derisive. The urban elite of a rigorously patriarchal power here gets feminized. But unlike the dignified goddess Roma, whose temples proliferated in the empire, Great Babylon is revealed, reviled, as the lowest possible grade of femininity: as sex slave. The great Unveiling turns into sadomasochistic strip show: in an apocalyptic flash its porn queen is humiliated, slaughtered, and devoured.

In our anachronistic dreamreading, the veils are still coming off. As the beast turns on the whore, the satire turns back to bite Revelation's own masculine purity. A host of feminist biblical critics have unveiled the sexism of the figuration of lascivious excess, and of course the demonization of sex workers.[16] But the

---

13. C. P Jones, "*Stigma:* Tattooing and Branding in Graeco-Roman Antiquity," *Journal of Roman Studies* 77 (1987): 139–55, here 151.

14. Moore, *Untold Tales*, 123.

15. Ibid., 115 (emphasis mine).

16. Luis Menéndez-Antuña, *Thinking Sex with the Great Whore: Deviant Sexualities and Empire in the Book of Revelation* (New York: Routledge, 2018).

biting master of apocalyptic reversal opens the parody to its own animal and sexual ambiguity: "One cannot say where the beast ends and the woman, Babylon, begins, since they each symbolize Rome." Moore thus infers that "the whore in combination with the beast represents Rome as the collapse of masculinity back into the morass of femininity and animality."[17]

The bestial parody keeps twisting. For does this fem-animal chaos not return us to the figuration of our first sign? It opened into very differently mingled sexes and species, gathering as in a cloud: with the wooly one "like a human" manifesting feminine breasts and then lamb's body. In the "hyperqueered figure of Jesus in Revelation, all hierarchical binaries dissolve—not only male over female and masculine over feminine but even human over animal. They are digested in his ruminant, ovine stomach and leak as milk from her human, female breasts."[18] What John might hear as Moore's satanic derision of his vision, we might also read with ironic appreciation—at once of the current queering and of the capacity of an ancient pornē-graphy to provoke it. From the vantage point of gender, queer, and animal studies, the smudging of celestial hierarchy into cloudy complication works its own unveiling. Sexual ambiguity is not as such the problem. As had the beast with horns and mortal wound, the slaughtered porn queen's drag version of masculinity performs its own mocking mimesis of the messianic body.

The fury with which the red beast turns on its orgiastic rider is not about sexuality. The vision meta-forces its sadomasochism to unveil something else, something fundamental, about the Rome complex, something for which there was then no straight vocabulary. We above recognized the Great Whore as code for the imperial economy. In narrating the self-destruction of a civilization, John is dreamreading, I suggest, something neither sexy nor

---

17. Moore, *Untold Tales,* 152.
18. Ibid., 152 n. 18.

dreamy: an internal contradiction between political power and global economics.

5. Political Horns, Economic Porn

The beast of multiple horns and heads encodes a multiplicity of nations and kings constituting the power of the Roman state. But the internationality of the empire is sustained by its global system of commerce, rendered by John as inhuman in its power. Horny monster and ostentatious rider are displayed partaking in the inebriating wine of injustice and bloodshed, in utter symbiosis. As routinely takes place between politics and economics? The state can offer political support, tax benefits, police and military backing for the economy, which in return rewards the politicians it rides. Power is prone to carry on its back insatiable wealth. In Revelation's political economy, the political sovereignty operates as global superpower, while the economic system—"seated on many waters"—reigns over an ancient global marketplace. Or market planet.

And now? The forms of political economy have shifted dramatically, through evolutions and revolutions, through various democratic, capitalist, socialist. . . . Sometimes for the better. Sometimes for the beast. Through the centuries of modernity the economic system of capitalism has grown and prospered, selling itself as the true mate of democracy. It lives from the correlation of the freedom of citizens with the freedom of markets. As capitalism grew ever more global, another sense of "freedom" emerged. Freedom *within* a nation state becomes inseparable from the freedom of capital to cross *beyond* national boundaries unconstrained. It makes the biggest profits by finding cheap labor—elsewhere. In this neoliberal model the inebriating union of wealth and power, in its mutual imbrication of capital and nation, begins to evince its contradiction.

Here we turn to a sober contemporary analysis of politics and economics (with aptly apocalyptic title): *How Will Capitalism End?* Wolfgang Streeck demonstrates that "capitalism has been on a crisis trajectory since the 1970's, the historical turning point being when the post-war settlement was abandoned by capital in response to a global profit squeeze." He found three long-term trends, "all starting more or less at the end of the post-war era and running in parallel, again, through the entire family of rich capitalist democracies: declining growth, growing inequality, and rising debt—public, private, and overall." This German economic sociologist, with no interest in U.S. religion or apocalyptic culture, cannot resist declaring that "the three apocalyptic horsemen of contemporary capitalism—stagnation, debt, inequality—are continuing to devastate the economic and political landscape."[19] (The fourth is oddly missing.)

Such recent economico-political trends cannot be extrapolated from John's harlot parody. But the wider pattern of the "crisis sequence" can be. Government policies in recent history "vacillated between two equilibrium points, one political, the other economic, that had become impossible to attain simultaneously. . . ." Current Western democracies, according to Streeck, are undergoing a dangerous struggle between two constituencies: the "national state people . . . and the international market people." The crisis comes to a head because capitalism "can only survive by constraint of its own complete commodification" of land, labor, and money. Yet it is motivated by infinite, insatiable "growth."

---

19. "To be precise, three crises followed one another: the global inflation of the 1970's, the explosion of public debt in the 1980's, and rapidly rising private indebtedness in the subsequent decade, resulting in the collapse of financial markets in 2008." See Wolfgang Streeck, *How Will Capitalism End? Essays on a Failing System* (Brooklyn, NY: Verso Books, 2016), 15, 18.

And there is no regulatory structure on the scene with the power to insist upon constraint. As the crisis took its course, "the post-war shotgun marriage between capitalism and democracy came to an end."[20] That 1945 marriage was made not in heaven but in the urgency of establishing a new order after the catastrophe of two world wars (make deals not war) and in the challenge of communist competition. In this century is the divorce looking even more like the break-up of John's whore-beast couple?

Still, you might object: the beast power does not signify any democracy, and capitalism bears little resemblance to its wanton ancestor. And what does the extremity of social contradiction in John's Rome have to do with a modernity that, disappointing though it proves, has nonetheless made, across a broad, slow range of statistics, significant democratic *and* economic improvements? Fair enough, especially across much of the socially democratic European nations. Yet consider a recent "Material Power Index" that compares the wealth of the top one hundred households in the United States to the bottom 90 percent; the ratio comes in at *108,765 to 1*. This, the study declares, "corresponds roughly to the difference in material power between a senator and a slave at the height of the Roman Empire."[21] Does such a continuum of oligarchic power from antiquity on not expose neoliberalism as neo-imperialism?

In the meantime, the "national state people"—often referred to as populists or neonationalists—have stormed into international prominence. "For those plotting to take advantage of growing discontent," writes Streeck, "nationalism appeared as an obvious formula both for social reconstruction and political success. The winners and the losers of globalism found themselves reflected in

---

20. Ibid., 16, 24, 20.
21. Jeffrey A. Winters, *Oligarchy* (New York: Cambridge University Press, 2011), 215, 217.

a conflict between cosmopolitanism and nationalism. . . ."[22] So we have seen the rise not just in the United States but in Europe of neonationalism—an international chain of movements recharging local identities through white supremacist hostility against immigrants.[23]

The *Rome*ness of the economic cosmopolis, that is, its city-hood, is a complex phenomenon. It includes freedoms of multicultural diversity (of racial, sexual, and religious difference), which in progressive thought often make common cause with critiques of capitalism. Yet it seems we have dangerously underestimated a crucial tension. "There is an almost insuperable cultural barrier between the city and the country. . . . City dwellers develop a multicultural, cosmopolitan outlook." Dangerous tensions then—now—develop between urban and rural populations. "Seen from the perspective of the provinces, elite cosmopolitanism serves the material interests of a new class of global winners. Mutual contempt is reinforced by self-imposed isolation, both sides speaking only to and within their camps. . . ." It is crucial not to confuse, however, the liberal elite metropole with a more radical intersectionalism—a cosmopolitanism with *cosmos*. (Here the Sunwoman signals. . . .)

As to that symptomatic red-orange beast (this does not take a head with wisdom) feeding on international business ventures, partly garishly visible, partly clandestine: it attacked both global trade treaties *and* the pluralist cosmopolitan ethos. "The Trump presidency," wrote Streeck soon after it began, "is both the out-

---

22. "The old left having withdrawn into stateless internationalism, the new right offered the nation-state to fill the ensuing political vacuum." See Wolfgang Streeck, "Trump and the Trumpists," *Inference: International Review of Science* 3, no. 1 (April 2017).

23. As Hannah Arendt predicted in her 1946 essay, "The Seeds of a Fascist International," in *Essays in Understanding (1930–1954): Formation, Exile, and Totalitarianism* (New York: Schocken, 2005).

come and the end of the American version of neo-liberalism."[24] Right-wing nationalism profits from international capital even as it protests it. An inebriating new vintage of antagonism fermented of sexed and raced resentment gets pressed from a working class neglected by liberalism and neoliberalism and directed by the talking image of fake news. What had we here, if not a globe-shaking internal collusion-and-contradiction of international nationalist politics and unconstrained global capitalism? Like a vulgar cartoon, do the Super Beast and Slut Supreme still ride?

Thus, for example, the runaway wildfires in California were not caused by climate change but by environmentalists: if they hadn't blocked the logging of those trees, there wouldn't be a problem. Truly the *pornē*-logic of one who "will know no grief."

6. Trumpocalypse Now and When?

Amidst treacherous lurches of contradiction, we will not want to lose track of the Christian fundamentalist vision of Babylon's internationalism. As a symptom of the U.S. religio-political right, the 2018 *Trumpocalypse*, with its account of the current Babylonian globalism, economic and otherwise, remains revealing.[25]

---

24. "Clinton's daring attempt to present herself as advocate of those Americans 'working hard and playing by the rules,' while collecting a fortune in speaker's fees from Goldman Sachs, was destined to fail" (Streeck, "Trumpists").

25. "Occupy until I come," the backcover shouts. By that phrase Luke's Gospel meant: hang in there until a time of justice and love becomes possible. Here, "Christians went to the polls, and God showed up. . . ." By the way, if anyone still wonders how, speaking of Satanic, the Trump of porn star associations and self-contradicting outbursts was so favored by God, the author offers the old answer: "King David was a murderer, liar, and adulterer, but he was the only man in the Bible whom God called 'a man after his own heart' (1 Sam. 13:14 KJV)." See Paul McGuire and Troy Anderson, *Trumpocalypse: The End-Times President,*

The book's subtitle summarizes the argument: *The End-Times President, a Battle against the Globalist Elite, and the Countdown to Armageddon.* Zooming in on that elite, the authors display "as one of the Bible's greatest mysteries" the tattoo on the great Pornë's forehead: "'MYSTERY, BABYLON THE GREAT, THE MOTHER OF HARLOTS AND OF THE ABOMINATIONS OF THE EARTH." She offers the key to the authors' "prophecy" of a "deep state coup and occult explosion." They reveal "how an interlocking network of transnational corporations, international banks, government agencies, think tanks, foundations, and secret societies is working to create a global government, cashless society, and universal religion as predicted by the prophets."[26] This all colludes in "the Great Deception."

U.S. fundamentalism from its nineteenth-century beginnings warned of the diabolic conspiracy for a one-world government with various spiritual heresies and international (read Jewish) banks.[27] But in their update, McGuire and Anderson present the globalization of the economy as now the primary guise of the harlot queen: "the evils of globalism, like abortion, deeply grieve the heart of God." (Nice touch, warming a rather abstract economic notion with women's wantonness.) "Trump," they declare triumphantly, "is one of the few politicians who is at war with globalism. Most of the Republicans and Democrats, along with Obama and the Clintons, for all intents and purposes, are on the payroll of the wealthy corporate elite. They sold America down the river

---

a Battle against the Globalist Elite, and the Countdown to Armageddon (New York: FaithWords, 2018), 36. For the opposite point of view, see David Frum, *Trumpocalypse: Restoring American Democracy* (New York: Harper, 2020).

26. McGuire and Anderson, *Trumpocalypse*, 97.

27. See Matthew Avery Sutton, *American Apocalypse: A History of Modern Evangelicalism* (Cambridge, MA: Belknap Press of Harvard University Press, 2014).

long ago—as did their EU counterparts—with numerous trade treaties that promote globalism."[28]

That last claim illustrates what Streeck laid out: the perceived fusion of political liberalism and economic neoliberalism. However, where he infers a perilously indeterminate outcome, these voices of the religious right offer excited certitude: "This is it. . . . This is our greatest moment. God specifically planned before the beginning of time for you to be here in America at this particular moment." You, reader! "Today, Babylon is rising again as the Luciferian order ascends. . . ." So expect "a world-wide economic crisis involving the crash of the dollar and a multibillion-dollar derivatives blowout. Also they quote a *New Yorker* article on "Doomsday Prep for the Super-Rich," showing that about half of Silicon Valley insiders are prepping for doomsday, stockpiling supplies, buying property in New Zealand, etc.[29] Unfortunately that is real. Along with this, among those left to fight it out for scarce resources, they predict—and may be on target here also—an America that explodes in "race wars." At the same time the "deep state" of all the intelligence agencies who plotted against Trump goes hand in hand with an occult plot being advanced by CERN physicists: all hidden in the Harlot's "mystery."

Trying to thwart the dawning of "the greatest supernatural awakening in human history," the cosmopolitan conspiracy is driven by "New Age beliefs" that the authors enumerate:

Everything—the earth, people, plants, and animals—is god.
Everyone can attain "Christ-consciousness."
Mankind is destroying the earth, and unless it changes,

---

28. "Trump opposes globalism" whereas "Hillary thrives on it" (McGuire and Anderson, *Trumpocalypse*, 98).

29. Ibid., 296; 12f.

"Mother Earth" will be forced to destroy humanity. The
biggest culprit of this destruction is Christianity because
the Bible says people have dominion over the earth. . . .
Jesus is just one of many great teachers, including Muhammad, Buddha, and Confucius.
Global peace will only be obtained through the New World
Order, a universal monetary system, and a one-world
leader.[30]

In this promiscuous spirituality, religious pluralism, theological liberalism, spiritual inclusivism, and environmentalism are
one: it is the evil of the "pan," the All, of pantheism—the perennial bugaboo of orthodoxy.[31] Any encompassing account of interdependence embraces the Whore of Wholeness. So the climate
science is as key to their demonology as was Darwin to the fathers
of fundamentalism. For this anti-science, anti-pluralist ideology,
notions of global public, global warming, fold together in the conspiracy of the global, liberal/neoliberal, elites. That none of this
apocalypse can be found, *literally* speaking, in the text that the
religious right purports to read literally has never mattered.

Still—though it grosses out my inner John of Patmos to admit
it—the specific reading of the countdown to Armageddon as a
"battle against the globalist elite" and so against a Satanically glo-
balized capitalism, does capture something of the text's prophetic
intuition. It also sharpens our awareness of the deep right *antagonism* to the presumed neoliberalism of elite *conservatives*. The contradiction between politics and economy cuts across party lines.
In its capacity to deliver much of the white working class and rural

---

30. Ibid., 117.

31. For a brilliant exploration of the fear and vilification of pantheism,
see Mary-Jane Rubenstein, *Pantheologies: Gods, Worlds, Monsters* (New
York: Columbia University Press, 2018).

population to the Republican Party the Christian right can read its politics as a virtuous rejection of the Global Harlot. But since it cannot recognize the beast of its nationalist politics, indeed of its "aspirational fascism,"[32] it is blind to its own apocalyptic self-contradiction. For the Porn Queen remains at once the funding source of the right and the consuming desire of much of the populist electorate—as in John not only the elites but most of the population of the conquered cities crave the luxury of "her dainties." So even as "she" rides the many-horned beast of a global nationalism, the Christian right shares the saddle.

For instance—and speaking literally—there is nothing more global than global warming. So *Trumpocalypse* can incoherently identify the environmental movement with the global economy that is *causing* the climate catastrophe. And the resentment of white fundamentalists can be weaponized on behalf of the globally (and locally) filthiest extractivism—to the profit only of the Babylonian elite. As the climate crisis increasingly reveals itself to swathes of the ecologically and economically vulnerable populace, denialism will gain in aggression.

7. Earth Matters

In the meantime, the fourth horseman missing in Streeck's glancing reference has trotted back in. The unlimited growth of the market is met by the limits of the "resource base." The matter of the earth will not neatly reduce to the stuff of dollar signs: it yields neither to the stuff of industrial capitalism nor to the postindustrial globe of pure finance. In the meantime the

---

32. William E. Connolly, *Aspirational Fascism: The Struggle for Multifaceted Democracy under Trumpism* (Minneapolis: University of Minnesota Press, 2017). See also William E. Connolly, *Climate Machines, Fascist Drives, and Truth* (Durham, NC: Duke University Press, 2019).

multitudes, pushed to multiply further by conservative birth policies, will need more and more matter. And yet the droughts and fires, floods, and extinctions will allow less and less of it. Matter Strikes Back. So pestilence also rides the pale green horse, making a mockery of the U.S. government. As levels of unemployment and desperation mount to once-in-a-century levels, revealing our self-destructive political economy, it gallops circles around our Harlot-ridden Beast: limits matter. Earth matter demands limits.

In the drunken voracity of "mystery, Babylon"—the incarnation of consuming greed as global economy—the political beast does not constrain her. He eats her up. But it is the same civilization consuming and being consumed, even as it consumes the lives of its laboring populations and the life of its planet. The self-commodifying harlot and the predatory power function together, or not at all. The beast therefore goes down too.

A certain Christian fundamentalism does at least recognize global economics as a threat, we noted. But in its theology globalization poses a threat *to*, not *of*, our species' dominance. Granted, at the first biblical appearance of the human a "dominion" was conferred. The priestly authors wrote the Genesis text of the creation under or just before conditions of beastly dominance by the original Babylonian Empire. Genesis 1:26f.—radical for its time—grants the dignity of creation "in the image of God" to all members of our species. That meant insistently: women, children, slaves. All of us, all together.

Theologically, then, what divinity, what divine quality, could we have been expected to reflect? Most evidently: Elohim creates. And so we are called to creativity. But what kind? The first chapter of Genesis is clear: divinity creates not from nothing but from "the deep." And then Elohim says, Good! To everything created, every shining, flowing, glowing, creeping, crawling, swimming, and, finally, speaking thing. Good! Good! So presumably we are called to emulate that love of the material universe. On the symbolic sixth day, after our emergence, "God saw *everything* that he had made, and indeed, it was very good" (Gen. 1:31). Humanity is not in itself "very good," despite the common misreading. We are "all in" with everything—all the matter of the creation. Otherwise we hardly matter.

What a beastly irony: somehow human god-likeness got taken as "go for it, godly world masters: use up the earth, waste its creatures." As we just about have. But not quite. The waters of primal chaos flow still: from a source, an alpha, opened before the romp of the pornē-beast pair. And after?

We aren't there yet.

6

Weaponizing the Word
A Tale of Two Suppers

Then I heard what seemed to be the voice of a great mul-titude, like the sound of many waters . . . and of mighty thunderpeals, crying out, Hallelujah! For the Lord our God the Almighty reigns.

—*Revelation 19:6*

Maybe there's a God above
But all I've ever learned from love
Was how to shoot somebody who outdrew ya

And it's not a cry that you hear at night
It's not somebody who's seen the light
It's a cold and it's a broken Hallelujah
Hallelujah
Hallelujah
Hallelujah.

—*Leonard Cohen*

1. Messianic Counterpoint

Around Christmas or Easter you can hardly avoid catching some burst of Handel's grand setting of Revelation 19:16: "Lord of Lords! King of Kings!" And yet hearing Handel's entire *Messiah*—

not just the Hallelujah Chorus but all three parts of the oratorio, live in Carnegie Hall—stunned me. I was unprepared for its affect of tender, yearning care. Part One opens not with the Apocalypse but with Isaiah 40:4:

> Comfort ye, comfort ye My people, saith your God.
> Speak ye comfortingly to Jerusalem,
> and cry unto her, that her warfare is accomplished,
> that her iniquity is pardoned
>
> The voice of him that crieth in the wilderness;
> prepare ye the way of the Lord; make straight in the
>   desert
> a highway for our God.

The selections do justice to the poetics of Hebrew hope.[1] Only after the choir sings its way through a long series of prophetic writings will Handel proceed to Jesus's birth: Part Two opens with a quotation from the Fourth Gospel—"Behold the Lamb of God"—and dwells upon the familiar image of comfort and gentleness. "Surely he has borne our grief and carried our sorrows." The music invites, amplifies, indeed *carries*, this work of shared mourning.

The settings lose their tender mood, however, as the selected texts expose the power structures of the world:

> Why do the nations so furiously rage together,
> and why do the people imagine a vain thing?

---

1. This still ubiquitous translation was commissioned by the King James who preceded Handel's patron James II. King James I reigned over Scotland and England from 1603 until his death in 1626; King James II ruled England and Ireland from 1685 until he was deposed in the Glorious Revolution of 1688.

> The kings of the earth rise up,
> and the rulers take counsel together against the Lord,
> and against His Anointed. (Ps. 2:1–2)

The warring nations thus find unity by directing their fury against the Anointed, in Hebrew *maschiach*, the hope of justice. In response, "Thou shalt break them with a rod of iron . . ." (Ps. 2:9). Only then, with ten Hallelujahs and an explosion of language from the Apocalypse—"for the Lord God Omnipotent reigneth" (Rev. 19:6, KJV)—comes the Hallelujah Chorus. "Lord of Lords!" Let the shrieking choral outcry mark also the arrival of this chapter's dreamcoded bit of the Apocalypse: the sixth, *the weaponizing of the word*. Its originative Jewish hope becomes audible: the yearning for a messianic age in which unjust rule would know itself overruled. The rulers of the earth would at last practice justice and mercy; they would recognize rather than expropriate that authority that is Lord over them.

At this live concert, something else took me off guard. The audience, secular, cosmopolitan, diverse (including Jewish friends in my company) sprang to its feet for the whole of the Hallelujah Chorus. That is the tradition, but in context I was startled to see such unhesitating respect. Something more than the righteous glory of the Apocalypse was coming through, something disarming even in its militancy. Yet that "more" had never long disarmed the lineage of lords and rulers (including those who commission such art).

Despite some great performances, have millennia of disappointments quashed the splendor of biblical hope? Even if the messiah arrived for the followers of Jesus, the messianic age did not. And has not. Christians have been waiting for him to "come again" almost as long as Jews had awaited the first. Yet it turns out there is in the Bible no "Second Coming."[2] To be literal: the hope

---

2. The only language approximating "second coming" in scripture

of Christ's "coming" does occur almost thirty times in the New Testament, but with no "again" or "second" attached: the term is *parousia*, which does not mean return. It means "presence." The biblical hope remains intriguingly less futuristic than its heirs. It isn't about someone who came, went, comes again—down, up, and back from a supernatural heaven. It looks to a radical presence, a being-now, never merely absent, and so never simply returning.

The ancient form of the messianic hope stirred by Jesus had been dashed for his community by the crucifixion. But the hope raised with him—in the psychosomatic visions of a few grieving friends, the resurrection as what Paul called the "spiritual body"—was no last word. Nor were the disappointments. Though the empire would continue to strike back, the prophetic dream of a collective resurrection—a great rising up spiritual and material—was recurrently revived.

In a musical tradition very different from Handel's, a jaunty spiritual opens with "Ezekiel connected dem dry bones." We sing along through the whole skeleton: "thigh bone connected to the hip bone, hip bone connected to the back bone. . . ."[3] Written a century ago, against the background of slavery and lynchings, the African American composer and author James Weldon Johnson was setting the prophet Ezekiel's vision of Israel, lying long dead in the "valley of dry bones." Even in the desert of white supremacism those bones at last come rattling back together: "Dem bones gonna rise again." The hope dreamreads ancient prophecy.

---

is Hebrew 9:28, which promises that Christ "will appear a second time, not to deal with sin, but to save those who are eagerly waiting for him."

3. See Helen Brown, "The Life of a Song: 'Dem Dry Bones,'" *Financial Times* (March 18, 2016), ft.com. For recent theo-homiletical use of this imagery, see Luke A. Powery, *Dem Dry Bones: Preaching, Death, and Hope* (Minneapolis: Fortress Press, 2012). See also the classic commentary on the genre, James H. Cone, *The Spirituals and the Blues* (Maryknoll, NY: Orbis Books, 1992).

Messianic expectancy had been strained already for centuries before the Christian epoch. And that hope would be further tested by the ongoing outbursts of state persecution of Jews who did and (post fourth century) who did not follow Jesus. The Apocalypse keeps particularly audible the messianic disappointment of the century following Jesus's brief life. The violence and the disillusionment cloud all hopeful breakthroughs since. Now in the third millennium after Jesus's birth, the hallelujah—once we leave the concert hall—might ring hollow. Not the collective comfort of a triumphal return, but global pestilence, poverty, and breakdowns of planetary health seem to await "the inhabitants of the earth."

To add heavenly insult to terrestrial injury: does not John's King of Kings bear some burden of culpability? It is not that the one who was expected simply failed to arrive. Someone, something, arrived in his name, over and over, with the galloping crosses of the Crusades, with the burning crosses of the KKK. Something kept coming again, and again, to the vigorous refrains of Christian violence.

Now, in a dissonant postmodern counterpoint, do we hear a "broken hallelujah" echoing after Handel's Choir—even as "dem bones" creak and rattle toward a percussive arising?

2. Schizopocalyptic Justice

Then I saw heaven opened, and there was a white horse! Its rider is called Faithful and True, and in righteousness he judges and makes war. His eyes are like a flame of fire.... He is clothed in a robe dipped in blood, and his name is called The Word of God. And the armies of heaven, wearing fine linen, white and pure, were following him on white horses. From his mouth comes a sharp sword with which to strike down the nations, and he will shepherd them with a rod of iron; he will tread the wine-press of the fury of the wrath of God the Almighty. On his robe and on his thigh he has a name inscribed, "King of kings and Lord of lords." (Rev. 19:11–16)

In a memoir reflecting on his struggle with bi-polar disorder, Mark Vonnegut points to a prior bi-polarity. "I also take issue with the idea that Jesus, after the Crucifixion and Resurrection, started working out and riding horses and having second thoughts about the Sermon on the Mount and the Beatitudes. Where did this new muscular Christ come from?"[4] Vonnegut trots us right back to Revelation, where the messianic figure we first spotted in the cloud now gallops in on "a white horse."

Here in this late chapter of the Apocalypse, the "rider is called Faithful and True." Sounds almost lamb-like, and evidently not identical with the God to whom he is faithful. But make no mis-take: "in righteousness he judges and makes war." The messianic warrior comes forth now in full force. No breasts protrude, no wooly hair morphs into sheep's head. "And the armies of heaven, wearing fine linen, white and pure, were following him on white horses." Their linen never gets bloody, though his—like the Lamb's coat—already is: "he is clothed in a robe dipped in blood, and his name is called The Word of God."

Another resemblance to the first sign: that tongue. "From his mouth comes a sharp sword with which to strike down the nations, and he will rule them with a rod of iron." One hint, again lost in translation, recollects the sheep: the Greek reads: "he will *shepherd* them." But then, "he will tread the wine press of the fury of the wrath of God the Almighty. On his robe and on his thigh

---

4. Mark Vonnegut, *Just Like Someone without Mental Illness Only More So: A Memoir* (New York: Delacorte Press, 2010), 163.

he has a name inscribed . . . 'King of kings and Lord of lords.'"
(Handel's lyrics omit that text with its inebriating bloodthirst and
the intimacy of the tattoo.)

Lord S/Word terminates the injustice of "the nations." Not
directly named Messiah, Jesus, Christ, or Lamb, this rider will
perpetrate the penultimate victory. So we had best again pause
and ask: Is this muscular Word of God "Faithful and True" to
the word of God named by the other John, the writer of a letter
that identifies God with love?[5] Or to the Gospel attitude of the
Beatitudes? Yet at the same time we ask: What social change, however loving, is ever brought about without sharp *words*? And then
when does that cutting edge, that eschatos, of activism, of confrontation, of visionary courage, harden into iron?

Storyline: the planet-wide battle of Revelation 19 defeats the
beastly superpowers. In the process, most of their subjects, not
just the elites, not even just Roman citizens, get slaughtered. At
the opening of chapter 20, the beast, his false prophets, and the
dragon-Satan are cast into the lake of fire to be kept there in torment for "a thousand years." That *chilia*, "millennium," has been
much anticipated ever since. There those who died in resistance
to Rome will be resurrected to rule "with Christ for [the same]
thousand years." After that, a brief final battle. At last the festivity
of the marriage of the Lamb can begin.

The chronology remains cloudy, nonlinear—appropriate to
dream-time. For actually "the marriage of the Lamb has come"
already, before the rider on the white horse (Rev. 19:7). It seems to
precede all the violence and the thousand years. So what will happen after the thousand years, upon the final release from "prison"
of the old serpent-dragon-devil-Satan? He deceives the nations

---

5. "Whoever does not love does not know God, for God is love" (1 Jn.
4:7).

again, gathers "Gog and Magog" (often identified as Islam) from "the four corners of the earth," surrounds the "beloved city"—but is consumed by fire from heaven. Then: final judgment and fullness of the new creation, which our last chapter will contemplate: the "holy city, the New Jerusalem, coming down out of heaven from God, prepared as a bride adorned for her husband." Is hers also a second coming? Remarriage? It seems rather that the visions themselves spiral in a dream parousia—putting the lie to the endless literalizations and calculations of events in linear sequence marching to the End.

We sympathize in this meditation with the narrative, amidst a hope-starved history, of a doom that leads to the happy ending of bride and groom. But with the righteous warrior in bloody white the Word of God has been weaponized. Even delinearized, there is no straight escape from its nightmare violence. We can only pass *through* it. That means facing, feeling, the text's conflict with itself. A dream (the German word is *Traum*) may reveal unhealed trauma—damage, tensions, contradictions that may crack into pathological schisms, into what at the collective level becomes schizopocalypse. Here disclosure closes against itself, unless the tension is—unsealed *as* unhealed.

We earlier encountered the internal tension in the binary of lamb and lion. The Lion of Judah, an emblem of royal power, signifies the longstanding hope, recurrent through much ancient Jewish history, in which John's faith steeps: that a great warrior king will come to save little Israel from its imperial enemies.[6] This hope for a final victorious confrontation shapes biblical eschatology, which gradually, a couple hundred years before the Christian era, turns more extreme, more dualistic in the opposition of good

6. Richard D. Patterson, "Lion and Lamb as Metaphors of Divine-Human Relationship," *Bible.org* (April 2, 2009).

and evil, more desperately dependent upon divine might; indeed, amidst more and terrible disappointments, more—apocalyptic.

As Jesus's followers, among them John of Patmos, wrestled with how to interpret his sudden gruesome death, resurrection did not simply solve the problem. Isaiah's alternative messianic figure, called "the suffering servant," was key to their discernments: "Like a lamb led to the slaughtering block, like a sheep silent before her shearers . . ." (Isa. 53:7).[7] John follows this nonviolent messianism; he means to "hold the testimony of Jesus." That means not to *worship* Jesus but: "Worship God! For the testimony of Jesus is the spirit of prophecy" (Rev. 19:10).

That prophetic spirit had yielded the image of an impossible coincidence of opposites: the lion lies down with the lamb. There Isaiah—already in the eighth century BCE—dreams an ultimate ecology, where the ferocity and the vulnerability of the messianic hope are reconciled. Anachronistically speaking, it seems our Darwinian aggression does not vanish but evolves into "hyper-cooperativity"—painted as vegetarian companionship with the long-suffering love-lamb.[8]

In the metaforce of Weaponized Word, however, it is as though the Lion returns as bloodthirsty "Word of God." The Lamb bloody

---

7. "Jeremias relates John the Baptist's words to the prophecy concerning the suffering servant foretold by Isaiah: 'He was treated harshly and afflicted, but he did not even open his mouth. Like a lamb led to the slaughtering block, like a sheep silent before her shearers, he did not even open his mouth' (Isa. 53:7)" (ibid.).

8. Marcia Pally, "Philosophical Questions and Biological Findings: Part I: Human Cooperativity, Competition, and Aggression," *Zygon* 55, no. 4 (December 2020): 1090–1106. For the relational underpinnings and theological implications of cooperativity, see Marcia Pally, "Separability-Amid-Situatedness or Distinction-Amid-Relation in Theological Voice," pt. II, chap. 1 in *Commonwealth and Covenant: Economics, Politics, and Theologies of Relationality* (Grand Rapids, MI: Eerdmans, 2016), 123–54.

from its *own* slaughter will retain its wooly nonhuman and non-violent manifestation to the very end of Revelation. Yet the text indirectly blends the Lamb and the (endlessly lionized) Judge and Warrior-Word. One must indeed ask: does not John render the victim one with the victorious victimizer? Has the bloodied Lamb become the bloody warrior? Never in the text. The Lamb is not directly identified with the warrior figure of this Word here named "King of kings and Lord of lords," this one who now "judges and makes war" (Rev. 19:11). "Jesus" as witness—the Greek term is *martyrion*—is to the end linked to the slaughtered Lamb, not merged with the warrior. That distinction does not solve the problem of Christian warfare; it does demand mindfulness of a dangerous paradox. Psychotheologically speaking, a bipolarity holds—one side does not defeat the other. It retains its schizopocalyptic tension.

The vision foregrounds the Lamb, which John "sees"; whereas he only "hears" the Lion who "has conquered." Even so, the irreducible difference of Lamb/witness/love and Lion/warrior/judge seems to be sustaining the chance of a transformative coinciding —if, in Cornel West's famous dictum, we never forget that "justice is what love looks like in public."[9] That just-looking love does not banish but reroutes power; the bloody Lamb doesn't roll over and play dead, or march to inevitable defeat. And it certainly does not sheepishly retreat to safer pastures. In the prophetic witness, justice never acquiesces in personal sentiment—always a temptation of love. Just love requires—it sees—a whole social order, a new world, a renewed "heaven and earth."

---

9. "To be human you must bear witness to justice. Justice is what love looks like in public—to be human is to be love and be loved." See Cornel West, *Hope on a Tightrope* (Carlsbad, CA: Hay House, 2008), 181, cf. 210.

3. A Tale of Two Suppers

> Then I saw an angel standing in the sun, and with a loud
> voice he called to all the birds that fly in mid-heaven,
> "Come, gather for the great supper of God, to eat the flesh
> of kings, the flesh of captains, the flesh of the mighty, the
> flesh of horses and their riders—flesh of all, both free and
> slave, both small and great." (Rev. 19:17–18)

Before we glimpse the new world, however, a further register of
traumatic symptomatology kicks in. It manifests in another tension of opposites—this one even more grimly satiric than John's
beast/whore parody. With another roaring "hallelujah!" like "the
voice of a great multitude, like the sound of many waters," we
hear that the Lamb's marriage has come. John is told by the angel:
"Write this: Blessed are those who are invited to the marriage supper of the Lamb." But soon an angel issues a different sort of dinner invitation to all the birds: "Come, gather for the great supper
of God, to eat the flesh of kings, the flesh of captains, the flesh of
the mighty. . . ." But that is only the main course.

Then: the "flesh of all, both free and slave, both small and
great." It seems that all who merely failed to risk their lives resist-
ing Rome—most of the human population—get killed by the rider,
with "the sword that came from his mouth; and all the birds were
gorged with their flesh." In this sneering satire, the joyous wedding
feast of the Lamb gets mirrored by the anthropophagic feast of
God. So—lives led in mere submission to the empire are worthless.
"For the birds." But I saw Hitchcock's *The Birds* at an impression-
able age. I cannot declaw the metaphor. The feast of horror seems
to be the shadow directly cast by the marriage supper.

The difference between the two feasts manifests not the integra-
tion of coinciding opposites but their schizopocalyptic contradic-

tion. In this scene Revelation does not just reveal an inevitability, but a *voracity* of divine violence facing systemic violence. The prophetic hope for a civic order symbolized by the bride, the coming New Jerusalem, gets here invested in genocide. Did John miss the radical gospel of his own guru: to love even the enemy? Indeed "love" as such is hardly an operative notion in the Apocalypse.[10] Unnamed, love does seem to drive the promised wedding of the Lamb—and unnamed, gets trumped by loveless power.

The tension of just love does not hold. But such pathological symptoms as the double supper do not let us either dismiss the text or apologize for it. Its ethically nightmarish scenes do not demotivate the dreamreading, they make it crucial. The messianic history carries within itself—within *our* histories—the unresolved tension between the healing hope and the gory glory. In that tension press the deep life frictions of peace and violence, of justice and vengeance, of love and fury.

Tempting though it is to toss the whole apocalyptic narrative "to the birds," that would only trap us in its mirror. What if we instead "hold the testimony," that is, hold it in consciousness? Then we may hold it responsible—able to respond. Not the same as *blame* it. John did not cause the voracious violence of empire, he mirrored and mocked it. He envisioned Roman injustice worsening—as it did, all too literally, over a century later, under Diocletian, in the largest and bloodiest persecution of Christians (303–311 CE). Neither did John's messianic violence *cause* the subsequent history of Christian Empire. Nor does Revelation's thousand-year rule of the martyr-saints account for the thousand(ish)-year reign of the Byzantine Empire (330 CE–1453). Surely not. . . .

Yet we must keep asking: did his text sanctify in advance the

---

10. John reads "love" as a disciplinary force: "I reprove and discipline those I love. Be earnest therefore and repent" (Rev. 3:19).

aggressions of Christian sovereignty? "It is a stupid clemency that spares the conquered foe."[11] So writes Bishop Eusebius, the great theological apologist for the first Christian emperor, justifying Constantine's mass executions of defeated "barbarians." The enemy is not to be ridiculously "loved" but stamped out. Righteously. Now that Christendom *was* the empire, did John's armies of heaven, his "feast of God," begin to operate as self-fulfilling prophecy? Did it produce an "apocalypse habit"—a voracious repetition of the final battle-doom-salvation scenario?[12]

Revelation's impact was helped by its canonical placement, exploding as it does at The End of the long Book of books, Scroll of scrolls. The twenty-seven books designated the New Testament got definitively canonized only two centuries after John wrote. John's Revelation was the last text to be included. It happened to be another leading theologian of Constantine's time, Athanasius, who in 367 finalized the list of authorized texts. It does not seem accidental that this canonization takes place just as Christianity ascends not only to freedom from persecution—a joyous "supper of the Lamb"—but at the same time to its own imperialization. The table was set for the "supper of God."

4. Religious Freedom or Christian Trophy?

If the Apocalypse was key to the Christianization of the empire, it was not innocent of the imperialization of Christianity. So a brief

---

11. Quoted in Ramsay MacMullen, *Constantine* (New York: Harper & Row, 1971), 40.

12. I did try to blame the text, reading it as a self-fulfilling prophecy—as though its violent vision was influential enough to have fueled the atrocities of later Christian power. That reading is not simply wrong, but it underplays the systemic violence that long preceded the Christian era: the imperial force that John's messianic Lamb/Warrior comes to defeat.

dive into this formative stretch of civilization will help to sort our current apocalypses.

Over a century before Eusebius, Athanasius, and Constantine, the African theologian Tertullian had been emboldened by the vision of John of Patmos to make an unprecedented demand upon Roman rule. This was something that "he might have been the first to conceive, an idea that American revolutionaries, more than fifteen centuries later, would incorporate into their new social and political system: freedom of religion, which Tertullian, writing in Latin, calls *libertate religionis.*" The historian Elaine Pagels tells how Tertullian argued for religious freedom—courageously confronting the Roman magistrate Scapula—as a "fundamental human right, a power bestowed by nature, that each person should worship according to his own convictions, free from compulsion."[13] In this way followers of Jesus widened the gap that Jews (under foreign rule) had placed between politics and religion. "What Tertullian demanded on the basis that God had created the human soul, American revolutionaries would claim on similar grounds, alluding to the Genesis creation account to insist, in 1776, that 'all men are created equal, and endowed by their creator with certain inalienable rights.'"[14]

The great African theologian was articulating the egalitarianism that would drive not only a (Christian) revolution against a later (Christian) empire, but also fuel the struggle for the emancipation of African slaves.[15] In a time when the white Christian

---

13. Tertullian, quoted in Elaine Pagels, *Revelations: Visions, Prophecy, and Politics in the Book of Revelation* (New York: Penguin Books, 2012), 131; Tertullian, *Apology*, 24; *To Scapula*, 2.

14. Pagels, *Revelations*, 132.

15. Laurel Schneider draws out a racially meaningful connection between Tertullian's originative construct of the Trinity and current struggles for a pluralist justice in her *Beyond Monotheism: A Theology of Multiplicity* (New York: Routledge, 2008).

right has commandeered the rhetoric of "religious liberty," this bit of ancient history wants to be unforgotten. Key to the present analysis, Tertullian was channeling the messianism of the Apocalypse. "Tertullian, of course, was speaking of freedom for Christians, and hoped for it only after Rome's downfall, when, as John had prophesied, Christ would descend in glory to reign over the New Jerusalem. But what actually happened was something that the fierce prophet John, for all his visions of the future, could hardly have foreseen."[16]

John had promised the triumph of the messianic S/Word over the multiheaded beast. But it was a Christian triumph *over* Rome he pictured—not the triumph *of* Rome *as* Christian. Irony of ironies: the beast of many heads morphs into the Lord of lords. Dreamreading the sign of the weaponized Word, we flash to the famous dream attributed to Constantine, on the night before a major battle against his rival. The dream advised him to "mark the heavenly sign of God on the shields of his soldiers ... [B]y means of a slanted letter X with the top of its head bent round, he marked Christ on their shields."[17] This sign is the *chi rho*, *XR*, the first two letters in Greek of *xristos*. In a different account, Eusebius describes a vision Constantine had while on the march: "He said that about mid-day, when the sun was beginning to decline, he saw with his own eyes the trophy of a cross of light in the heavens, above the sun, and bearing the inscription, 'Conquer by this.'"[18] "Trophy" refers to cruciform banners on which was imprinted the

---

16. Pagels, *Revelations*, 132.

17. Lactantius, *De Mortibus Persecutorum*, 44.4–6, in *Lactantius: De Mortibus Persecutorum*, trans. J. L. Creed (Oxford: Oxford University Press, 1984), quoted in Noel Lenski, "The Reign of Constantine," chap. 3 in *The Cambridge Companion to the Age of Constantine*, ed. Noel Lenski (New York: Cambridge University Press, 2006), 71.

18. Eusebius, "The Life of the Blessed Emperor Constantine," vol. 1 in *The Greek Ecclesiastical Historians of the First Six Centuries of the*

XR. Behold the first army to march, *liter*ally, under the letter of Christ.

Constantine's victories folded what was then a three-headed Roman Empire, prone to violent rivalries, into one, making him sole Caesar. In 324 he moved the capital from Rome to Byzantium, which he renamed Constantinopolis ("city of Constantine"), also called *Nova Roma.* While no convert until his deathbed, he recognized the potential of the Christian movement, which kept spreading despite recurrent persecutions, to consolidate his regime. He passed a law that prohibited the persecution not only of Christians, but (give him credit) of *any* for their religion—the policy that Tertullian had advocated a century before.

If you had been a follower of Jesus at the time, would you not embrace this stunning shift? Would you not have welcomed this foretaste of the wedding supper of the New Jerusalem? Over the long stretch of Constantine's reign, apocalyptic signs multiplied. On one coin is engraved the defeat of the dragon, with the cross as trophy. A painting of the time fleshed out the role of Constantine as the warrior lord, triumphant over a Satanic sea dragon. Eusebius praised the emperor's brilliant realization—conceptual and political—of John's Revelation: "and I am filled with wonder at the intellectual greatness of the emperor, who as if by divine inspiration, thus expressed what the prophets had foretold concerning this monster. . . ."[19] Rome had always been harsh. But as displayed in coins, sculpture and oratory, "the gulf between We and They deepened, the ruler and his armies rose higher above a

---

Christian Era (London: Samuel Bagster & Sons, 1843–1847), bk. 1, chap. 30, p. 27.

19. Eusebius Pamphilus, *Church History, Life of Constantine, Oration in Praise of Constantine,* Nicene and Post-Nicene Fathers ser. II, vol., 1, ed. Philip Schaff; trans. Arthur Cushman McGilffert (Grand Rapids, MI: Wm. B. Eerdmans, 1890), bk. 3, chap. 3.

hapless enemy, all cruelties were excused, all 'barbarians' lumped together."[20] No "stupid clemency" there. Toward such recalcitrant ethnic others of empire, wholesale slaughter and enslavement of populations proceeded. Dinner for the newly adopted God?

One wonders how church leaders at the time interpreted the unmistakably anti-Roman thrust of the Book of Revelation. How in their context of a newly Christianized empire did they handle its anti-imperialism? This is where Athanasius's theology came into play. His collaboration with Constantine worked because both sought a unifying orthodoxy. There were among Christians divergent interpretations of Christ's relation to God— was he of the "same" nature (*homo-ousios*) or a "similar" one (*homoi-ousios*)? That (literal) iota of difference was not confined to scholarly debate but famously fueled communal disputes and spilled into street brawls. Constantine didn't care (one iota) about theological nuance. He convened the Council of Nicaea to unify Christianity as a bulwark for the unification of the empire. One Lord, one empire, one emperor, one creed, one faith, one baptism. Athanasius's party beat that of Arius, whose "*oi*" was henceforth heresy (though note that there were no executions over dogma, just some exiles). The Nicene Creed has framed the doctrine of most churches since.

What, then, of Athanasius's reading of Revelation? "Athanasius reinterpreted John's visions of cosmic war to apply to the battle that he himself fought for more than forty-five years—the battle to establish what he regarded as 'orthodox Christianity' against heresy." To this end, Pagels explains, he reads Revelation's cosmic war as a vivid image of his own battle against heretics. He thus deploys John's visions as sharp warnings to "Christian dissidents:

---

20. Ramsay MacMullen, *Constantine*, Routledge Revivals (New York: Routledge, 2014; orig., Dial Press, 1969), 40.

God is about to divide the saved from the damned—which now means dividing the 'orthodox' from 'heretics.'"[21]

In the fourth-century metamorphosis of the Roman Empire, the anti-imperialism of Revelation's S/Word retreats to the margins. The schism between orthodoxy and its heretical foes (who also believed themselves orthodox, "right-thinking") would deepen into an intra-Christian abyss. But it is only at the end of the century, under the emperor Theodosius, that Christianity became the official state religion. Then persecution of other religions as well as of alternative Christian confessions was rendered not only legal but normative. The quick swerve from religious freedom into religious persecution echoes eerily in the deployment today of "religious liberty" to suppress practices (especially pertaining to sexuality, often as practiced by other Christians) deemed non-Christian. Religious liberty on the Christian right thus operates under the banner of the *chi rho*—fusing social, legal, and political powers with presumed theological orthodoxy.

5. Onward XR Soldiers

As imperial power grew new heads in the West, vested in the Roman papacy, new enemies provoked novel forms of religio-political unity. This becomes nowhere more explicit than in Pope Urban II's launch of the Crusades against the Muslims one thousand years ago: another pattern not yet outgrown. A smart political theologian, he implored Christian nobles to fight against the "true enemy," rather than against each other: "Let those who have been fighting against their brothers and relatives now fight in a proper way against the barbarian."[22] "Europe" as such arguably

---

21. Pagels, *Revelations*, 165.
22. Citied in Roberta Anderson and Dominic Aidan Bellenger, eds., *Medieval Worlds: A Sourcebook* (New York: Routledge, 2003), 90.

emerged from its internal warfare by unifying against this external foe.[23] Islam, as dissident younger brother of the sons of Abraham, could then also be cast as a heretical and political threat. The legal theorist of the Third Reich, Carl Schmitt, deemed such a "friend-enemy distinction" the first principle of all politics. "Tell me who your enemy is and I will tell you who you are."[24]

The point here is not that the S/Word has fought only on the side of Christian empires. Movements that arose in dissent *against* the new politico-religious form of Roman hegemony were also emboldened by Revelation. For instance, they read in the Great Whore the obscene wealth of the papal city. These movements were inspired by the recorded visions, dense with apocalyptic allusions, of the twelfth-century monk Joachim of Fiore. He announced the imminent breakthrough of the "Age of the Spirit" when church hierarchy would fall away, as all would have direct access to God. All goods would be held communally, as in the agapic communism of the first generation of Christians. As these movements—radical Franciscans, Waldensians, Bohemians, Hussites—spread, the church recurrently denounced them, along with innumerable Jews and "witches," as heretics. Inquisitions and massacres were Christ-sanctified.

It was only with the Protestant Reformation that protest against Rome succeeded *politically* and could therefore survive *religiously*.

---

23. For more, see Catherine Keller, "Crusade, Capital, and Cosmopolis," chap. 8 in *Cloud of the Impossible: Negative Theology and Planetary Entanglement* (New York: Columbia University Press, 2015), 239–65.

24. Carl Schmitt, "Theory of the Partisan: Intermediate Commentary on the Concept of the Political (1963)," *Telos* 127 (2004): 85. "[T]he specific political distinction to which political actions and motives can be reduced is that between friend and enemy." See Carl Schmitt, *The Concept of the Political*, exp. ed., trans. George Schwab (Chicago: University of Chicago Press, 2007, 1996), 26.

Luther was able to channel the nationalist discontent of the German princes with the Holy Roman Empire into the radical break from its church.[25] Now John's political anti-imperialism returns full force. About the Apocalypse, however, Luther remained deeply ambivalent. "About this Book of the Revelation of John, I leave everyone free to hold his own opinions. . . . I say what I feel. I miss more than one thing in this book, and it makes me consider it to be neither apostolic nor prophetic."[26] In one historian's paraphrase: "go with your gut, Luther says, in so many words."[27] Luther knew as a scholar that it was not "apostolic" (written by the author of the Fourth Gospel), and believed it should not have been canonized. He complained that it failed to speak plainly, dealing instead with "visions and images." After all, for him "the ears alone are the organs of a Christian. . . ."[28]

Yet Luther's brilliant translation of the Bible into colloquial German did nothing to diminish interest in its last book—with its "visions and images." For he included no fewer than twenty-one full-page illustrations of its scenes, based on woodcuts by his friend, the court painter in Wittenberg, Cranach the Elder.

---

25. For example, an image used in the 1545 edition of Luther's Bible shows the Whore of Babylon wearing the papal tiara (figure 6). For more on Luther's comparison of the Whore of Babylon to the Roman Catholic Church, see Martin Luther, "The Babylonian Captivity of the Church, 1520," ed. Erik H. Herrmann, in *The Annotated Luther: Volume 3: Church and Sacraments*, ed. Paul W. Robinson (Minneapolis: Fortress Press, 2016).

26. Martin Luther, "Preface to the Revelation of Saint John," in *The Works of Martin Luther*, vol. 35: *Word and Sacrament: Volume One*, ed. E. Theodore Bachmann (Minneapolis: Fortress Press, 1960), 398.

27. Timothy Beal, *The Book of Revelation: A Biography* (Princeton, NJ: Princeton University Press, 2018), 121.

28. Martin Luther, "Lectures on Hebrews," in *The Works of Martin Luther*, vol. 29: *The Selected Pauline Epistles, Volume 2*, ed. Jaroslav Pelikan and Walter A. Hansen (Minneapolis: Fortress Press, 1968), 224.

Lucas Cranach the Elder, *The Whore of Babylon Illustration for the Luther Bible*, 1522. Collection of The British Library, London.

Cranach's images curated the Apocalypse "as an overwhelmingly visual encounter."[29] The influential force of the images of the Great Harlot wearing the papal tiara can hardly be underestimated.

The metaforce of anti-Roman protest fueled an early modern anti-imperialism, religious and nationalist. Amidst the social turbulence Luther had reason to worry that apocalyptic motifs can backfire. Thomas Müntzer, leading a new radical wing of the Reformation, was like prior radicals prophetically inspired by Joachim's reading of Revelation. Müntzer confronted the injustice of the German princes against the peasants, and finally led them in armed revolt. Luther, however, depended upon those princes to make possible the dangerous split from Rome. Now he supported, with the fury of the S/Word, the princes' slaughter of 100,000 peasants. Hear Luther's weaponized Apocalypse: "Let no

29. Beal, *Revelation*, 123.

one think that the world can be ruled without blood; the sword of the ruler must be red and bloody; for the world will and must be evil, and the sword is God's rod and vengeance upon it." In this vein Luther also authored *On the Jews and Their Lies* (1543).[30] The tragic irony of the schizapocalypse deepens.

The Reformation evinces one more deep symptom of what Gil Anidjar all too astutely diagnoses as "Christian hemopolitics."[31] "Blood is the name and the thing that does and undoes the significant concepts of the Christian world, the distinctions that divide Christianity from itself: theology from medicine, finance from politics, religion from race, and so forth."[32] Eucharistically sanctified and shared, flowing from Christian empires East and West into the early modern racializations of "the bloods" and into apocalyptic bloodfeasts all along—blood drenches Christian history. It poisons all bodies of Christian faith (like John's bloodied seas) that do not *mind* their, our, bloodthirsty legacies.

As the fury of the Lord got wine-pressed by Protestant principalities and powers, it was answered with Catholic vintages. What could be shared between Christians was more blood. In terms of proportion of the population massacred, the Thirty Years' War counts as the bloodiest in Western history.[33] Later religiopolitical violence against other others—Jews, indigenous, and enslaved peoples, communities of women healers accused of witchcraft— would drive the carnage toward its properly apocalyptic globality.

---

30. Martin Luther, "About the Jews and Their Lies," in *The Annotated Luther,* vol. 5: *Christian Life in the World,* ed. and trans. Hans J. Hillerbrand (Minneapolis: Fortress Press, 2017), 440–607.

31. Gil Anidjar, *Blood: A Critique of Christianity* (New York: Columbia University Press, 2014), 84.

32. Ibid., 258.

33. Steven Pinker, *The Better Angels of Our Nature: Why Violence Has Declined* (New York: Penguin, 2012), 195.

The birds of the modern centuries were assured a gorge-orgy of great diversity.

I do not want to keep marching us through the historical mimicries of "the great supper of God." You might think secularization would finally put a stop to it. That would depend on *which* secularization: In other words, what kind of theology is getting secularized? Concerning the past century's secularization of apocalyptic genocide, a poster series marches into view. Enlistment posters from Vichy under Nazi occupation translate Constantine. One features French troops in the uniform of the Reich over the tagline *Sous ce signe vinquerons.* Under this sign we will win. Constantine's cross twisted into swastika. Another substitutes the SS-bolts.

Waffen SS recruitment poster 1943. "With your European comrades under the sign SS you will conquer."

The origin of the phrase Hitler popularized, "the thousand-year *Reich,*" was obvious to European Christians: "and they will reign with him a thousand years" (Rev. 20:6). More directly, the Nazis appropriated Joachim's influential vision of 1135: his Third Age, or "realm," is in German "Third Reich." And yet. Joachim's third realm of the Spirit had inspired the *anti*-authoritarian movements, communalisms, proto-communisms, and spiritual countercultures of Europe.

For all this: the old scroll of the Apocalypse, even in its messianic extremities, is neither the primary cause nor deep motivation of Constantinian imperialism, of early modern nationalism, or later fascism. The patterns of superpower precede and exceed John's text. But the Weaponized Word could always be deployed to render oppression righteous, annihilation noble, and slaughter inevitable. In order to avoid such many-headed evil it remains therefore tempting to take the stance of an anti-apocalypse.[34] But do we not then mimic in reverse the dualistic purity of the Apocalypse? Better to mind it than to mirror it.

6. *Revelations, Revolutions*

The difficult irony running through each of our signs, even, or especially, this militant one, can be summarized in this way: the history of collective *resistance* to oppression is no less an effect of the Apocalypse than is the oppression itself. Behind John's double-edged vision operates the Jewish messianism that leaves traces in all modern progressive movements. A twentieth-century voice of prophecy captures its legacy thus: "What is at work here is the longing for that rightness which, in religious or philosophical vision, is experienced as revelation or idea, and which of its very nature cannot be realized in the individual, but only in human community."[35] As Martin Buber in his advocacy of a utopian

---

34. For more on "anti-apocalypse," see "Opening: Dis/closing 'The End,'" chap. 1, and "Time: Temporizing Tales," chap. 3, in Catherine Keller, *Apocalypse Now and Then: A Feminist Guide to the End of the World* (Boston: Beacon, 1996; reprint, Minneapolis: Fortress Press, 2004),

35. Martin Buber, *Paths in Utopia* (New York: Collier/Macmillan, 1949), 7.

socialism demonstrates, that longing for rightness (far from self-righteousness) begins with the primal I–thou relation. It matures into community rimmed with eschatological possibility. When eschatology intensifies as apocalypse, the way is opened for systemic change—and with it, always, the risk of a violently unifying dualism of us versus them.

Ernst Bloch, the East German philosopher of the same period (who had to flee to the West when his Marxism and atheism no longer convinced the authorities), wrote the history of hope itself. He tracks the social force of hope from the Hebrew prophets on through its apocalyptic rendering in the "Christian social utopias."[36] "Thus a single line runs from the half-primitive communism remembered by the Nazarites to the preaching of the prophets against wealth and tyranny, and to the early Christian communism founded on love."[37] His great three-volume *Principle of Hope* pivots around Joachim of Fiore, whose millennium-old visions burn with "an anger born of hope . . . which had hardly been heard since the days of John the Baptist." Hope does not live severed from the rage for justice. "They deck the altars, and the poor man suffers bitter hunger," wrote Joachim. We noted the historic consequences of this "most momentous social utopia."[38]

Bloch's secular Jewish embrace of the monastic visionary Joachim rings with a double anachronism (from him back to Joachim, and from our post-communist present back to socialist Bloch), even as it unearths the deep apocalyptic sources of revolution. Joachim's importance consists in his having transformed the traditional "trinity of mere *viewpoints* into a threefold gradation *within* history

---

36. Ernst Bloch, *The Principle of Hope*, vol. 2, trans. Neville Plaice, Stephen Plaice, and Paul Knight (Cambridge, MA: MIT Press, 1986), 515.

37. Ibid., 497.

38. Ibid., 498.

itself." The three Persons become three epochs dynamically over-lapping: of the Father/authority, the Son/sibling, the Spirit/friend. The Third Age of the Spirit—radically egalitarian—aspires to an agapic communism derived from the early Christian social utopia of Acts. "Connected with this, and with even more momentous consequences, was the complete transfer of the kingdom of light *from the other world and the empty promises of the other world into history. . . .*" Bloch points forward to the Joachite influence in Bohemia, Germany, Russia, then England: "Only the heretical sects, with Joachim among them, allowed revelation to spring up anew even in the West; and the Holy Spirit accordingly recommended astonishing Pentecosts to them. It recommended social principles of Christianity which . . . were not cringing and did not treat the proletariat as a rabble." Bloch honors the spiritual emergence of the secular revolutionary movements. He goes on to cite the young Engels's stimulation, only a few years before the *Communist Manifesto*, of apocalyptic effects: "The self-confidence of humanity is the new Grail around whose throne the nations jubilantly gather." Setting the medieval Grail myth in Revelation's throne room, Engels solicits deep European reverb: "This is our vocation: to become the Templars of this Grail, to gird our swords about our loins for its sake and cheerfully risk our lives in the last holy war, which will be followed by the millennium of freedom."[39]

In a later millennium, progressives may say hallelujah to the courage to take up arms on behalf of collective liberation. But most of us do cringe at the actual outcomes of actual "holy wars." The "suppers of God" get served from Constantine on, through the Crusading slaughter of over ten thousand of the Muslim and Jewish inhabitants of Jerusalem in 1099. . . . Then nearly a millennium later, those sword-girded loins righteously slaughtered twenty million at the Soviet supper of Stalin. With Stalin, remem-

---

39. Ibid., 510, 515.

bered as "the grey blur," any distinction of justice and vengeance is erased.[40] The lion devours the lamb.

Perhaps now the left can only come into its own as it minds its own tension between militant nonviolence and holy war. Then it keeps conscious the totalitarian traumatism; it grieves the messianic disappointment that is state communism. And still there is no historically honest way to sever the ancient prophetic hope from the bloody Western revolutions, democratic or socialist. By the same token Joachim's momentous dreamreading of John's millennium lives also in the artful resistance practiced by nonviolent movements of the last few centuries. We glimpsed above his Third Age under the sign of the Sunwoman, in such experiments as that of the Quakers, the Shakers, the Universal Publick Friend (who could not have known of Joachim's Age of the Spirit as Friend). The linked political movements for the enfranchisement of women and for the emancipation of slaves were themselves full of millennial hope, charged with apocalyptic allusions—and productive illusions.[41]

---

40. In March of 1917, just months before the revolution, "Stalin had not turned forty. He was, then, just Stalin. . . . At best an adequate intellectual, at worst an embarrassing one. He was neither a party left nor a party right per se, but something of a weathervane. The impression he left was one of not leaving much of an impression." Sukhanov, chronicler of the Russian Revolution, "would remember him as 'a grey blur.'" China Miéville, *October: The Story of the Russian Revolution* (New York: Verso Books, 2018), 97.

41. "'Pealing! The clock of Time has struck the woman's hour, / We hear it on our knees.' All crimes shall cease, and ancient wrongs shall fail; / Justice returning lifts aloft her scales, / Peace o'er the world her olive wants extends, / And white-robed Innocence from Heaven descends." See Beryl E. Satter, "New Thought and the Era of Women: 1825–1895," PhD diss., Yale University, 1992. Regarding the emancipatory apocalypse, the great voice of Black liberation theology, James H. Cone, puts it thus: "Black slaves also expressed their

These nineteenth-century millennialisms, as secular movements with strong Christian support, were shadowed by the development of a diametrically opposed apocalypse: that of U.S. Protestant fundamentalism. Its "premillennialism" literalizes the struggle for the thousand-year reign of Christ by promising the "rapture" of born-again Christians. As noted earlier, apocalyptic expectation was all too literally weaponized in the formation of the religiopolitical conservatives who elected Ronald Reagan and, with him, expected nuclear exchange by the end of (the last) millennium. In the meantime that right wing has cultivated a huge, privately armed public. If fundamentalism has been fumbling about theologically in this century, it remains *right*-on politically. It increasingly replaces thoughtful versions of evangelical theology with "Foxangelicalism."[42]

None of the progressive movements in the West (and much of Asia) can get free of the prophetic messianism that spawned them. Nor can any of these historic movements be said to have in any final sense "succeeded." Religious antecedents, like the Waldensians, radical Franciscans, Bohemians, Radical Reformation, were cut down firmly and early. Some survived in dissemination and indirection. Their traces are not negligible—consider, for example, the promising effects of a pope in our epoch taking the name

---

anticipation of God's new future with apocalyptic imagination. 'Where shall I be when the first trumpet soun'; soun' so loud till it woke up de dead?'" See James H. Cone, *The Spirituals and the Blues* (Maryknoll, NY: Orbis Books, 1991), 46.

42. To be sure, there is a shifting spectrum of evangelical varieties, including an ever-growing evangelical left; "The Varieties of American Evangelicalism," *USC Center for Religion and Civic Culture* (November 1, 2018), crcc.usc.edu. See Catherine Keller, "Foxangelicals, Political Theology, and Friends," chap. 11 in *Doing Theology in the Age of Trump: A Critical Report on Christian Nationalism* (Eugene, OR: Cascade Books, 2018), 89–100.

of Francis and mobilizing that saint's radical spirit of solidarity with the earth and the poor.

We are also speaking here of vastly diverse secular trends whose anti-establishment force is rent with layers of internal tensions as to aim and strategy. The division within the early Social Democratic Party of Germany, for example, which in 1933 broke into its liberal and its Marxist wings, tragically made possible Hitler's ascendency.[43] Yet since the war that party's integrations of democratic and socialist impulses have institutionalized much progressive social and environmental policy. Or consider the opposition between the divergently messianic visions of Martin Luther King and Malcolm X—speaking of lamb and lion. The tension between them was profound—but, as theologian James Cone argues, also key to the transformative energy of the civil rights movement.[44]

Progressive hopes have not ceased to suffer disappointment—but has apocalyptically sourced revolution simply failed? Don't see any evidence dem bones gonna rise again?

7. Vengefeast or Lovefest?

To dreamread the S/Word of the Apocalypse means neither to cringe at its endless failures nor to enact its violence. It does mean to cut open a history of liberative messianicity, of deep democracy, and of revolutionary change, of intersectional social movements, even of a cosmic bent toward justice. And in the very opening irrupt present tensions, new contestations right there at the edge, the eschaton, of transformation. Where they hurt the most.

---

43. Gary Dorrien, *Social Democracy in the Making: Political and Religious Roots of European Socialism* (New Haven: Yale University Press, 2019), chap. 4.

44. James H. Cone, *Martin and Malcolm and America: A Dream or a Nightmare* (Maryknoll, NY: Orbis Books, 1991).

Solidarity in "the spirit of prophecy" will not arise from some solid common ground. The ground itself trembles: How can—just for instance—white, middle-class, science-driven environmentalists fighting to protect nonhuman species effectively team with anti-racist activists fighting for oppressed humans? And hey, isn't the common denominator economics? Or is it the common dominator? What about—us queers? Crips? And Me Too, still? Precisely because of its pluralist and planetary proclivities, the progressive spectrum is more vulnerable than the right to contradictions between its ever-apocalyptic priorities. Our differences can work either closure or disclosure. Even the terms of pluralism become problematic—some would exclude all religion (present book included) for the sake of a democratic secularization; others, for that same sake, work to include nonexclusionary forms of religion.

The dreamreading hope is to hold the "to come" true to its own messianic spirit: even when the shadow-side of the Apocalypse sticks out its sword-tongue at that hope—at its unrealistic dreams, its impossible egalitarianism, its progressivism without progress, its unprofitable appeal to the earth. The mindful apocalypse must tend the shadows. The prophetic spirit had once promised to turn the sword into the earth-keeping ploughshare, after all.

In the meantime, the spirit requires griefwork. For all those that the S/Word couldn't or wouldn't or will not save, for the losses multiplied, multiplying, beyond knowability. For the betrayals of the ancient hope of radical renewal. Over and over, hope's new beginnings got trumped and its traumas normalized. What does it mean to grieve these wasted worlds? To waste away in tears? Or maybe instead—after whatever tearful cleansing may flow—to refuse to veil the waste.

Grief may then rightly turn outward, turn to outrage. The problem is not "the fury of the wrath." Rage can energize resistance and change. But whenever the inviting lovefeast is preempted by the victorious vengefest, the spirit of justice goes down to another defeat. The transformative tension splits into we-good, you-bad. Then revolution slides toward final solution, the deep shadow of Revelation. So the schizopocalypse keeps shuddering through the history of radical aspirations and messianic disappointments. And even those shudders have shaken open new actions, new chances.

In present history, however, the shudder is shaking the very Earth—that figure who had opened her mouth so generously. As the Mourning Bird sang it, time is running out, and taking our space with it. Space is running out, and taking our time with it. John wrote of such a transition: "The earth and heaven fled from his presence, and no place was found for them." In contemporary words: "Entire worlds have ended before but never before the entire world."[45] That entirety does not mean universe or even planet. Just the habitable world, the earth habitat of ourselves, our cosmically entangled, dangerously gifted, achingly diverse selves.

Mere closure, after all? Lessons of pestilence, politics, and planet-wide pathos learned too late? The remains of the second supper, tossed to the birds? A last chance to "outshoot somebody who outdrew ya"?

Cold and broken hallelujah. Nonetheless a hallelujah.[46] The case of the ancient future is not closed. Comfort ye my people.

---

45. John Thatamanil, "Enlarging Our Love: Or How to Become Christians Who Truly Belong to the Earth," sermon, St. Philip Anglican Church (November 10, 2019), published at inaspaciousplace.wordpress.com.

46. "The 'cold and a broken hallelujah' is an exaltation—even one broken by breaches, chill, and doubt—of one lover for another, be it person or God." Marcia Pally, *From This Broken Hill I Sing to You: The Theology of Leonard Cohen* (London: Bloomsbury Academic, 2021).

7

Down to Earth
City, Tree, Water

> *rock upon rock*
> *charred earth*
> *in time*
> *strong green growth*
> *will rise here*
> *trees back to life*
> *native flowers*
> *pushing the fragrance of hope*
> *the promise of resurrection*
>   —bell hooks, "Appalachian Elegy"

> *And I saw the holy city, the New Jerusalem, coming down out of heaven from God, prepared as a bride.... And I heard a loud voice from the throne saying, "See, the home of God is among mortals...."*
>   —Revelation 21:2

1. Coming Down

When John, like the prophets before him seeking deep social and natural renewal, "saw a new heaven and a new earth," it is a *city* that rivets his attention. Becoming the Lamb's life-partner, this New Jerusalem brings home the dream—and the God—of a festively fresh start, a "new creation." Weddings were the big parties of ancient communities. Coming down "radiant like a very rare jewel," this ancient future city will climactically unveil the "new creation."

Quite a come-down from her to here, isn't it? Where fashionable billionaires and billions of fossil-fueled lights do most of the urban glittering?

And yet. However failed or fragmentary, forgotten or frumpy, the Bride City of the Apocalypse remains the most influential utopia in history. It sparkles across the secularreligious spectrum of messianic yearning for the materialization of a new community, a common planet, a better world. Hope for a "good place," *eu-topos*: it always downloads some trace of that fabulous future that never was, the gleaming city premodern or postapocalyptic. As we stagger into the third decade of the third millennium of the Christian era—the era of the unrealized expectation of the early Christian communities—has utopian hope lost all credibility?

Utopia quietly left the Lamb for another messiah: modernization. The West's faith in Man's Progress has, however, delivered the Anthropocene devastation of the human habitat. And in Christian *anti*-modernism, the New Jerusalem degraded into fundamentalist prep not for a better world but for rapture *out* of the world. Might as well use this world up: so the modern and the anti-modern currently collude in the political ecology of late capitalism. Its monetized earth, parceled into real estate for urban sprawl and rural desolation, still glitters with centers of glamor, town and country, the utopias for the deserving few.[1] Some of the

---

1. According to Naomi Klein, such utopias for the few are hinted at in plans for "Puertopia," whereby northern entrepreneurs profit from hurricane Maria's devastation of Puerto Rico. "Puerto Rico finds itself

wealthiest are also preparing more northerly estates, "doomsday prep" for the hotter times which their investments are bringing on. If the very space for a planet-scaled *good place* seems to be running out, it is not just because there are so many humans, and then more, but because so few have gained control of the *goods*.

The languishing life of the land and of the seas, altered chemistry of "the heavens," extinction of species, disappearing glaciers and flooded coastlines converge with the coming hundreds of millions of climate migrants.[2] Their coming will amplify racist, nationalist, and denialist politics. In the new global dance of death, *climatic* scale dwarfs the climactic scene of *The Seventh Seal*, where the local victims of medieval plague, holding hands, follow Death in a dignified dance of distinct personae. I hope the current enactment of pestilence on a mass scale will, as you read, have passed. But I fear that the scale of our imbalances with other humans and with nonhuman others will not have. So thinkers tuned to the topics of climate and the "tropics of chaos" are offering anything but utopian alternatives.[3] Hope for the future appears increasingly as a whitewashing of the present.[4]

---

locked in a battle of utopias." See Naomi Klein, *The Battle for Paradise: Puerto Rico Takes On the Disaster Capitalists* (Chicago: Haymarket Books, 2018), 78. Klein juxtaposes the post-catastrophe, gated Puertopias of capitalist Aynrandian bitcoin paradise for outside millionaires to the solar-paneled organic communities linked through hurricane Mariana. On doomsday preparations see, for example, Evan Osnos, "Doomsday Prep for the Super-Rich," *New Yorker* (January 23, 2017), newyorker.com.

2. As today, literally, I last-draft this chapter, the *New York Times Magazine* headline reads, "The Great Climate Migration." See Abram Lustgarten, "The Great Climate Migration," *New York Times Magazine* (July 23, 2020), nytimes.com.

3. See Christian Parenti, *Tropic of Chaos: Climate Change and the New Geography of Violence* (New York: Nation Books, 2011).

4. Miguel A. De La Torre, *Embracing Hopelessness* (Minneapolis:

How at this point could the gussied up New Jerusalem appear as anything but ancient fake news? An uncoming future for an unbecoming civilization? The good place is running out of time. The good time is running out of place. Who is that singing: "He's a real nowhere man, sitting in his nowhere land. . . . Isn't he a bit like you and me?"[5]

Is the good place nowhere land?

2. Downfall or Downcoming

It turns out the word "utopia" signifies first of all "no place," the meaning Thomas More intended when he coined the term for his 1516 book *Utopia*.[6] He wanted no confusion of his imagined ideal with any actual place. He also knew the Greek words for "no" (*ou*) and "good" (*eu*) are pronounced indistinguishably. So what is the relation of "no place" to "good place"? Is utopia always nowhere? Is the good place ever a real-life place? Or is it an ideal, a hope, that only works by negating the status quo?

A millennium and a half earlier, Revelation's cataclysmic preparation for the appearance of New Jerusalem is captured thus in the original: "the earth and the heaven fled from [God's]

Fortress Press, 2017). Consider also the brilliant work of thinkers who call themselves Afropessimists. For example, see Frank B. Wilderson III, Saidiya Harman, Steve Martinot, Jared Sexton, and Hortense J. Spillers, *Afro-Pessimism: An Introduction* (Minneapolis: Racked and Dispatched, 2017), rackedanddispatched.noblogs.org.

5. The Beatles, "Nowhere Man," side 1, track 4, on *Rubber Soul* (Capitol, 1965, vinyl).

6. Thomas More coined the term in Greek and wrote the book in Latin: The title *De optimo rei publicae statu deque nova insula Utopia* is literally translated, "Of a republic's best state and of the new island Utopia." See Thomas More, "Utopia," trans. John P. Dolan, in *The Essential Thomas More*, ed. James J. Greene and John P. Dolan (New York: New American Library, 1967).

presence, and no place was found for them" (Rev. 20:11) "No (*ou*) place (*topos*)": the very Greek words that will merge as "utopia." That verse is typically taken to mean that the original earth and heaven are being put out of their misery, annihilated, thereby making room for the new creation and its capital city. In this view God, who created the world out of nothing, now reduces it back to nothing. Clean sweep, *tabula rasa*. Floccinaucinihilipilification. (What, you don't know the longest English word, which combines four Latin terms for "nothing" to signify "the action or habit of estimating as worthless"?[7]) The cycle of creation from nothing, return to nothing, and new creation from nothing has deep reverb in Christian history. Yet there is no biblical creation or new creation from mere *nihil*.[8] And the interpretation of the no-place of Revelation as mere annihilation only amplifies later disdain of the natural universe. In recent decades it has provided religious justification for climate science denialism: if the Lord is about to terminate the world anyway, what's the point of trying to clean it up or cool it down? He'll make us a brand new one real soon.

A dreamreading of "no place" beckons urgently. If in context, before God's throne, "no place was found" for heaven and earth, is this because the creation itself is now deemed unworthy, the earth judged and doomed along with the human malefactors, hopelessly tainted by all things carnal? Certainly in John's geocentric vision the creation has suffered grievous harm. A radical restart is called for—hence the ancient metaforce of the new creation, of a "new heaven and new earth." Yet in his vision we saw Earth come

---

7. "Floccinaucinihilipilification, n.," *OED* Online (June 2020, Oxford University Press).

8. I summarize the scholarly consensus against any biblical *creatio ex nihilo* and offer instead a *creatio ex profundis* in Catherine Keller, *Face of the Deep: A Theology of Becoming* (New York: Routledge, 2003).

to the rescue of that cosmic Sunwoman. We heard "the destroyers of the Earth" condemned. So how could it suddenly be time for *God* to destroy the earth—indeed, the creation? But if not, why does the creation find "no place" before the throne?

Might it be because John is dreamreading a mysterious change of God's *own* place? Or more precisely of the human *understanding* of God's place? As we will see, the entire movement of our seventh sign can be summarized as a "coming down out of heaven from God." Yet God is at this festive moment revealed to be— already down there. A voice "from the throne" booms: "See, the home of God is among mortals" (Rev. 21:2ff.). Does the move of God *cum* Lamb into the New Jerusalem seem to signal a shift not of literal place but of spiritual viewpoint? The divine, in other words, here gets revealed as immanent to the world. It is no longer found dwelling *above* as most of the tradition before and after presumes, but "dwelling with them" (Rev. 21:3b)—cohabiting. Might that radical shift of perspective explain—in dream logic—why no space was found for them "before the throne"?

The very meaning of divine space shifts: the creation no longer reads as something *beneath* the creator. For the creator lives *within* the creation: within earth and heaven. Even inside the city: "the throne of God and of the Lamb will be *in* it" (Rev. 22:3). If New Jerusalem has become the new throne room: so of course there is "no place" for heaven and earth *before* the throne, as the throne is *within* heaven and earth. Sky, earth, city are revealed, renewed, as *God's place:* theotopia. The divine place *is* cosmic space. That makes the creation not identical to, but intimate with, its creator—who "will wipe away the tears" of mortals.

Such radical immanence of the creator to the creation would have been stunning to John himself. His was not a theism of mystical communion but of prophetic confrontation, presuming a God above confronting us below. So the metaforce of this divine immanence in its new cosmopolis is glimpsed dreamily. This theo-topology anticipates much later intuitions of immanence, of panentheism or of spirit within all things. God's indwelling is coded in the celebratory downcoming that is at the same time the descent of the bride-city to join the groom-lamb. (We don't hear if the blood gets washed off his white coat for the wedding.) The three are "coming down to earth." There occurs here no so-called "rapture," no upward sucking of the "saved" out of the earth.

The triune downcoming takes place in answer to the prior downfall. This apocalyptic celebration dis/closes a future beyond the horrific collapse of the global imperium—and its trinity of beasts. The prior ecopolitical fall of Babylon/Rome will have cleared the space—brutally, to be sure, with the weaponized words of mass destruction—for "those who conquer" rather than suffer "the second death." Yet the healing vision pushes through nonetheless. The cosmic metamorphosis does not happen smoothly, as though from nothing—or through inevitable progress.

The theotopic take-away seems to be this: collective transformation takes *place* with the dramatic shift away from the picture of God ruling, Caesar-like, from above.[9] Only as divinity "comes down" into intraworldly immanence can this new creation happen.

Perhaps most important: this making-new takes place not as a *replacement* but as a *renewal* of our actual place. It signifies a radical restoration of the natural world, not a supernatural substitution. It happens only through the chaos of the struggle of affirmative against destructive forces within history. God speaks—for the first time since the opening chapter—to say, "See, I am mak-

---

9. Excellent recent analyses of the broad New Testament resistance to Caesar include Stephen D. Moore, *Empire and Apocalypse: Postcolonialism and the New Testament* (Sheffield: Sheffield Phoenix Press, 2006); and Joerg Rieger, *Jesus vs. Caesar: For People Tired of Serving the Wrong God* (Nashville, TN: Abingdon Press, 2018).

ing all things new" (Rev. 21:5). This is far from the numbing presumption that God simply produces a whole new universe to take the place of the old one. Revelation is not about making all new *things* but making all things *new*.[10]

Apocalypse unveils divine immanence as a radical shift in perspective—not as a metaphysical change of God's "nature." The mystical interiority is, however, not absorbed in a private spirituality. Its spirit permeates the world. In and out, up and down, human and nonhuman, creator and creation, can no longer be held in simple opposition. The divine is the very place of the universe: hence one of the Hebrew names for the Unnameable One is *Makom*, the Hebrew for "place." Indeed divine immanence present in the female city may bear yet another register of mystical meaning. Jürgen Moltmann recognizes in and *as* this place God's *Shekinah*, the Hebrew feminine noun for "presence." "God's Shekinah is omnipresent and traverses all spatial borderlines."[11] In the medieval Jewish mysticism of the Kabbalah, this femininity is personified as the female Presence of God accompanying the Jews in their exile—an aspect split off from the He-God above. For the kabbalistic legacy it was the duty of every Jewish couple to reconcile the Unnameable One with "his" Shekinah (and to enact the reunion sexually every Sabbath).

In the Apocalypse also it was to be a celebratory spousal eros that embodies the divine immanence. Not that one finds here any

---

10. "The driving force behind the new creation is perhaps best summed up with the divine declaration in Rev. 21:5: 'Behold, I am making all things new' (cf. Is. 43:19). God does *not* say, I am making all new things. In the new creation, God is not starting all over again, creating from nothing after everything has been destroyed." See William P. Brown, *Sacred Sense: Discovering the Wonder of God's Word and World* (Grand Rapids, MI: Eerdmans, 2015), 149.

11. Jürgen Moltmann, *The Coming of God: Christian Eschatology*, trans. Margaret Kohl (Minneapolis: Fortress Press, 2004, 1996), 115.

fix for biblical heterosexism. The femininity of the New Jerusalem is not presented as an alternative to masculine rule, but to the feminized slut-city Babylon. And yet feminist scholarship avers: "The choice for the good woman that the author of Revelation wants us to make is not a gendered choice nor an individualistic choice but rather a political choice. It is the choice for God's *polis*, God's alternative city of justice and well-being."[12] And as we will see, of a rebalanced ecology, for a cosmopolis of God, a cohabitation rich in cosmos.

3. Alpha and Omega

And the one who was seated on the throne said, "See, I am making all things new." Also he said, "Write this, for these words are trustworthy and true." Then he said to me, "It is done! I am the Alpha and the Omega, the beginning and the end. To the thirsty I will give water as a gift from the spring of the water of life." (Rev. 21:5–6)

If the *eschaton* cannot be read bluntly as The End, it is because it dis/closes the dynamic *edge*. On the edge—of time, of world— there is unveiled an indiscernibility between what is ending and what is trying to begin. So the first and last books of the *Biblios* also come into new relation. While John had no notion that his document would be the last bit of a really big scroll, one can see why this placement proved irresistible to the Christian canonizers. It lets the Bible unfurl from the creation, through all knowable history, to the promised new creation. But does this mean that the events of Revelation stand at the end of the line of all

---

12. Barbara Rossing, *The Choice between Two Cities: Whore, Bride, and Empire in the Apocalypse* (Harrisburg, PA: Trinity Press International, 1999), 165.

time? Or does the Bible come full circle back to its beginning? Or then again, perhaps neither line nor circle?

The God who had spoken in the first chapter to say "I am the Alpha and the Omega" now speaks again in the end: "I am the Alpha and the Omega, the first and the last, the beginning and the end." So in this insistently nonlinear temporality, Genesis and Apocalypse seem to name the two edges of one being, one becoming, one process of creation. But the first and the last do not become the same. They *coincide*. At its omega point the creativity of genesis (the Greek word for "becoming") reveals itself as *regenesis*. The apocalyptic regeneration of the earth and the atmosphere, and so of the creatures that they house, takes place within a new experience of the divine indwelling.

As metaforce this divinely good place remains—then, now—in an important sense *no* place: it is a vision of *sheer possibility*. In process theology the content of the divine vision for the world consists of pure possibility—an infinite spectrum of possibility. In the political philosophy of Marcuse utopia also "functions as a negation of current actuality. The no-place of utopia doesn't ever come about. But it does draw a contrast with what is."[13] Without such an edge of contrast—often a sharply negative edge—we cannot imagine the really new possibility. The novum gets then reduced to some predictably or probably coming time. And such projection only confuses possibilities with concrete actualizations. That is what Whitehead calls "the fallacy of misplaced concreteness": the tendency to mistake the possible for the already actual.

Generative possibilities cluster like the dreams of what might or might not become. They come shrouded in clouds like the opening sign of Revelation. They may appear as elemental forms,

---

13. Thanks to Hunter Bragg for his reflection on Herbert Marcuse, *Counterrevolution and Revolt* (Boston: Beacon, 1972), chap. 3, "Art and Revolution," 79–128.

symbols with immense persistence even amidst their cloudiness. Indeed certain elemental images at the end of the Apocalypse must be dreamread in their mirror play with Genesis. But the New Jerusalem offers no restoration of Eden, nothing like return to a wilderness paradise—or to the prior oceanic chaos.[14] So the elemental forms connecting the gentle wilds of Eden with the glittering urban future are all the more striking.

> Then the angel showed me the river of the water of life, bright as crystal, flowing from the throne of God and of the Lamb, through the middle of the street of the city. On either side of the river, is the tree of life with its twelve kinds of fruit, producing its fruit each month; and the leaves of the tree are for the healing of the nations. (Rev. 22.1–2)

A tree, a river.

4. Tree of Life. Still.

A tree grows in a quieter edge of our present meditation. There in an earth-margin where optimism finds no ground a darker hope takes root: right in the no-place of our not-knowing. And now all at once, in insistent synchronicity, the tree branches into the following seven scenes: the recurrence of Eden's "tree of life" in

---

14. That in Apocalypse "the sea was no more" seems to eliminate the waters of Gen. 1:2. For John the sea represents the horror of invading Roman fleets as well as the greed of the marine trade. See Craig R. Koester, *Revelation: A New Translation with Introduction and Commentary*, Anchor Bible (New Haven: Yale University Press, 2014), 803. See also Micah D. Kiel, "Revelation's Upbringing: Critique of Empire and Its Ecological Components," chap. 3 in *Apocalyptic Ecology: The Book of Revelation, the Earth, and the Future* (Collegeville, MN: Liturgical Press, 2017), esp. "The Sea, the Sea," 78ff.

the New Jerusalem; an activist network named for the strangest tree on earth; a magnificent tree-novel; a nonfiction massacre; ecosalvation by reforestation; the tree monk; and the dark God "of a hundred roots."

(1) We hear from John of a single tree of life. But in the Genesis narration we read that every tree that was pleasing aesthetically or nutritionally got planted in Eden, though only two get named. One is the "tree of life," which has neither prohibition nor invitation attached to it. It is the other, the "tree of the knowledge of good and evil," which comes with the "do not eat" sign. When its fig (the supposed "apple") gets transgressively munched, it brings on mortality. That signifies, according to Paul Tillich, *consciousness of* mortality and so the "fall into freedom," whereby humans outgrow our "dreaming innocence." Tikva Frymer-Kensky links Eve not with Pandora, but with Prometheus.[15]

John's tree does not grow in a new Edenic wilderness but at the urban heart of the new—the renewed—world. Will it have been growing the whole time? Or will it be a seedling in a brand new "garden city," as Moltmann calls it, an "ideal of ecological city civilization"?[16] Nature and culture are herein reconciled. Yet how natural is the New Jerusalem, where "there will be no more death." After much agonized digesting of the knowledge of good and evil, a collective re-arising is promised—as it was from Ezekiel on, not for isolated or disembodied individuals but as the resurrection of shared life. It can be literalized as a supernatural afterlife. Or it can be dreamread in its context: then this radical restart of life signifies freedom from the fear of death. It cannot happen outside the force-field of "judgment" that somehow takes all lives into account, lives

---

15. Tikva Frymer-Kensky, *In the Wake of the Goddesses: Women, Culture, and the Biblical Transformation of Pagan Myth* (New York: Free Press, 1992), 109ff.

16. Moltmann, *The Coming*, 315.

not equally culpable for the fates of the earth but all immortalized in their particularity in "the book of life," all accountable.

At this point in the narrative, John of Patmos had already tossed all carriers of evil into the lake of fire, thus fueling the Western imagination of the inferno (truly, the pits). But now it is as though the pits of the fruit of the original tree become rich compost for the new earth, where there will be fresh sproutings. Radical arisings. From the root *radix*.

(2) There is something odd, however, about the singularity of Revelation's tree: "On either side of the river is the tree of life." Thus Stephen Moore's mordant take-down of the new city: "a continent-sized shopping mall with a single tree." Given the embrace by the religious right of Health and Wealth Gospel consumerism, the satire is all too apt. And yet how can a tree grow on both sides of a river? It must be at least two. William Brown argues that the Greek signifies here a collective singular.[17] As I might say, "The oak thrives on our campus. Hundreds of them."

And it is here that another image pops up. There lives an actual tree in Utah that is its own collective singular. It has a proper name, *pando populus*. Its root system is an immense rhizome: it supports thousands of quaking aspen trunks over a hundred square acres. It is also the oldest known tree, indeed perhaps the oldest, as well as the largest, living organism in the world. Its root system is estimated at 80,000 years. Ancient enough to symbolize arboreally the Alpha and Omega. *Pando* also figuratively solves

---

17. Brown notes that "the singular word 'tree' is used collectively in Greek to designate a grove or forest" (William Brown, *Sacred Sense*, 148). John is recalling not only the tree in Genesis but the tree in Ezekiel's vision (Ezek. 47:12: "on the banks, on both sides of the river, there will grow all kinds of trees") in which the Hebrew for tree is also singular but given the context suggests multiple trees.

the riddle of a single tree on "both sides of the river": such a rhizomatic system could potentially cross beneath rivers.

As it happens, *pando populus* lends its name to a Los Angeles–based activist network working to interlink multiple social justice and ecological movements—the brainchild of John B. Cobb Jr.[18] The process theologian has worked for over half a century to find alternatives to the global economics of climate change. Process theology envisions a cosmos arising moment by moment out of the relations between every register of existence. In its activism, secular and religious, it fosters the branching of its vision into collective material practices, toward "ecocivilization."[19] Ecociv: the *civis*, city, in healing symbiosis with its plurisingular Tree of Life.

(3) Like a great tree, Richard Powers's novel *The Overstory*—in which seventeen tree species are named on the first page—begins by branching into numerous subplots like short stories. They gradually grow into an arboreal immensity of entanglements. One plotline follows a little girl who loves trees more than people. Patricia becomes a botanist and spends years alone in forests doing her research. First she is ridiculed by her peers and much later celebrated, for a stunning discovery: trees are communicating with each other, all the time, by way of a nuanced chemical language transmitted from root to root.[20] Her expert testimony

---

18. Pando Populus, pandopopulus.com. Having survived endless natural catastrophes, the tree itself is now threatened by anthropogenic shifts of environment moving at incomparably faster speeds than its own life.

19. Inspired by the environmental philosophy of John B. Cobb Jr., the Institute for Ecological Civilization was co-founded by Philip Clayton and Wm. Andrew Schwartz to promote the long-term well-being of people and the planet through civilizational change. See EcoCiv.org.

20. Barbara Kingsolver writes of *The Overstory*: "Trees are everywhere but incidental, it seems, until the seventh tale in the series, about an odd little girl who loves trees more than she loves most people

at a trial opens the eyes of a skeptical judge: "I never imagined!" he marvels. "Trees summon animals and make them do things? They remember? They feed and take care of each other?"[21] Patricia's revelatory botany not accidentally anticipates now scientifically legitimated work of this century.[22]

The ancient Tree of Life makes its direct appearance late in the book, as a Vietnam vet turned radical tree activist, now in jail, listens to a tape of Patricia lecturing:

> The prof returns to her one great theme, the massive tree
> of life, spreading, branching, flowering. That's all it seems
> to want to do. To keep making guesses. To go on changing,
> rolling with the punches. . . . She describes an explosion
> of living forms, a hundred million new stems and twists

---

and grows up to be a scientist. As Dr. Pat Westerford she spends years alone in forests doing her research, initially mocked by her peers but eventually celebrated for an astounding (and actually real) discovery: A forest's trees are all communicating, all the time, via a nuanced chemical language transmitted from root to root. As this revelation dawns, the reader is jolted with electric glimpses of connections among characters in the previous stories. And then we remember we're in the hands of Richard Powers, winner of a genius grant, a storyteller of such grand scope that Margaret Atwood was moved to ask: 'If Powers were an American writer of the 19th century, which writer would he be? He'd probably be the Herman Melville of 'Moby-Dick.'" Barbara Kingsolver, "*The Overstory* by Richard Powers," *Environmental Ethics*, April 16, 2018, envirojpo.blogspot.com.

21. Richard Powers, *The Overstory: A Novel* (New York: W. W. Norton, 2018), 283.

22. Powers's character Dr. Pat Westerford resembles the plant ecologist who first researched how trees communicate, Dr. Suzanne Simone of the University of British Columbia. See also the German author, arborist, and forest ranger Peter Wohlleben, *The Hidden Life of Trees: What They Feel, How They Communicate: Discoveries from a Secret World* (Berkeley, CA: Greystone Books, 2016).

from one prodigious trunk. She talks about Tane Mahuta, Yggdrawil, Jian-Mu, the Tree of Good and Evil, the indestructible Asvattha with roots above and branches below. Then she's back at the original World Tree. Five times at least, she says, the tree has been dropped, and five times it has resprouted from the stump. Now it's toppling again, and what will happen this time is anybody's guess.[23]

This is a reference to the five great extinction events that have already occurred, starting 440 million years ago; and to the sixth mass extinction currently underway[24] (666 bleeping in the background). The totality of the anthropocene topple, or how efficiently our economics will trump environmental correctives, remains "anybody's guess." Having eaten the fruit of the tree of the knowledge of good and evil, our species both recognizes the evil and continues it.

The topple effect is far from total. Nor can its epochal ecology be read in abstraction from its immediate politics. It branches into interhuman trauma.

(4) I spoke of those arboreal interlinkages at a conference. While I was on my way home the Tree of Life Synagogue in Pittsburgh suffered its massacre.[25] Eleven dead. I was long booked for

---

23. Powers, *Overstory*, 491.

24. "Biologists suspect we're living through the sixth major mass extinction. Earth has witnessed five, when more than 75% of species disappeared. Paleontologists spot them when species go missing from the global fossil record. . . . 'We don't always know what caused them but most had something to do with rapid climate change,' says Melbourne paleontologist Rolf Schmidt." The first known extinction event was 444 million years ago. See Viviane Richter, "The Big Five Mass Extinctions: Extinctions Where More Than 75% of the Species Disappears!" *Cosmos: The Science of Everything* (July 6, 2015), cosmosmagazine.com.

25. "Armed with an AR-15–style assault rifle and at least three handguns, a man shouting anti-Semitic slurs opened fire inside a

an event in that very city, that same week. The dark synchronicity let me visit the site, in its neighborhood of flamingly beautiful fall foliage. I stood next to a colleague from Germany who was trembling in quiet horror at this new manifestation of anti-Semitism. While the shooting need not portend a new Holocaust, it does stir the traumatic memory of the Shoah.

The Tree of Life massacre is not alone; it expresses the racist violence blasting through the land. The symptom has not killed the Tree of Life. It exposes its vulnerability. The Tree sways nightmarishly. The final word of *The Overstory*—"STILL"—invites a subterranean quiet of mourning. And still the synagogue carries engraved on its building, next to the name "Tree of Life": *Or L'Simcha*—"the light of joy."

(5) This we now know: "Planting billions of trees across the world is by far the biggest and cheapest way to tackle the climate crisis, according to scientists, who have made the first calculation of how many more trees could be planted without encroaching on crop land or urban areas." How does this salvation by reforestation work? "As trees grow, they absorb and store the carbon dioxide emissions that are driving global heating. New research estimates that a worldwide planting program could remove two-thirds of all the emissions that have been pumped into the atmosphere by human activities, a figure the scientists find 'mind-blowing.'"

Resistance to reforestation will *not* be mind-blowing, even as we learn that deforestation has not only worsened the atmosphere's fever, but enabled the coronavirus pandemic. Destruction of

---

Pittsburgh synagogue Saturday morning, killing at least 11 congregants and wounding four police officers and two others, the authorities said. Campbell Robertson, Christopher Mele, and Sabrina Tavernise, "11 Killed in Synagogue Massacre; Suspect Charged with 29 Counts," *New York Times* (October 27, 2018), nytimes.com.

forest habitats leads to unsustainable cross-species relations (in this case with bats).[26] Nor can sufficient reforestation happen fast enough, even if "we" tried to stop the destructive two-degree C warming. Nonetheless the green healing of much of our habitat remains—not impossible.

(6) Long before that last study was released, my friend the tree monk had written from her island: "As I understand it, we humans have two very direct and effective actions for working on climate change—reforestation and building up the tilth and humus of soil." We heard in chapter 3 of her permaculture practice. "We can all get on board with these actions; both are effective carbon sequestration strategies."[27] Both pertain to how—after the Edenic hunter–gatherer millennia—we grow our food. Most deforestation has proceeded in the interest of agriculture. In modern times, that meant increasingly aggressive monocropping. "The human palate can be directed toward the work of regenerative agriculture, which tends the well-being of the soil in ways that industrial scale monocultures cannot—though even industrial monocultures can be better done (with cover crops, lower tillage) as we turn the huge ship of the human diet!" And crucially, reforestation is also for cities, especially in tree-barren, low-income, disproportionately black and brown neighborhoods, with implications for local and immediate, as well as planetary, health.

(7) An old friend just put into my hand Rilke's *Book of Hours*.[28]

---

26. Maciej F. Boni et al., "Evolutionary Origins of the SARS-CoV-2 Sarbecovirus Lineage Responsible for the COVID-19 Pandemic," *Nature Microbiology* (July 28, 2020), nature.com.

27. Sharon Betcher, permaculturing ecofeminist theologian extraordinaire, email correspondence with author (September 9, 2019).

28. Rainer Maria Rilke, *The Book of Hours: Prayers to a Lowly God,* bilingual edition, trans. Annemarie S. Kidder (Evanston, IL: Northwestern University Press, 2001). Thanks to Ignacio Castuera for passing this German and English version to me at the right moment.

One of its poems meditates on the Titian-like glory of "God Almighty marching in bliss." Then the poet swerves away from that weaponized apocalypse, disclosing a spirit far from John's theology but not from his plurisingular tree:

> And yet however much I lean into myself
> My God is dark and like a web
> Of a hundred roots, drinking quietly.[29]

This God had always already come down to earth. In the dark depths it imbibes—with no bloodthirst—the world. From the young Rilke's journal: "Nothing personal is to remain.... We empty ourselves, we surrender, we unfold—until one day our gestures are found in swaying treetops and our smile is resurrected among the children who play underneath these trees."[30]

5. Divine Immanence and the Healing of Nations

Of the tree growing on both sides of the river, we hear that it offers "twelve kinds of fruit, producing its fruit each month . . ." (Rev. 22:2). Once the tree(s) reveals their multiplicity, the dozen varieties of its yearly yield makes more botanical sense. But it is the political edge of John's parable that is delivered by the final clause: "and the leaves of the tree are *for the healing of the nations.*" As the trauma of the past chapters was collective, global, so is the healing dreamwork, *Traumwerk*, of these medicine leaves.

"The nations" clearly do not signify an afterlife or supernatural heaven. Lights went off for me when my colleague Wesley Ariarajah made this point in a sermon in the Drew chapel. John is

---

29. Rilke, *Book of Hours,* 4f., translation mine.
30. Ibid., 68.

envisioning an altered but recognizable world civilization, one that exhibits vestiges of a pre-imperial political polity. The healing spirit materializes multinationally. The tree of life had similarly appeared in the Jewish apocalyptic text of Enoch, where its eschatological healing power is emitted as the fragrance of its leaves: "[The tree's] fragrance will be in their bones, and they will live a long life on the earth, such as your fathers lived also in their days, and torments and plagues and suffering will not touch them."[31]

John was dreamreading a new multiplicity of nations, finally at peace in their differences. The internal multi-ethnicity of the twelve tribes of Israel prefigured such a possibility. Healed of the pornē-beast imperialism—and also, in this metaforce, of John's vengeful desires—the nations here branch into a healthy planetary life. Might they yet grow, after some noble and disappointing attempts at a just cooperativity, and despite Christian nationalist hatred of internationalism, into a leafier league of nations? A multiplicity in league even with the trees of the earth? Somehow plurisingular like the trees—not just one empire, not just a warring plurality—in this cosmopolitan vision? But these connections only work because of a profound, if rarely noticed, theological shift.

Under the sign of New Jerusalem, the plurality of earth's peoples cannot be separated from the immanence of divinity to the

---

31. 1 Enoch 25:6, trans. Eric J. Gilchrest, in *Revelation 21–22 in Light of Jewish and Greco-Roman Utopianism* (Boston: Brill, 2013), 245. "The importance of 1 Enoch 24–25 for understanding the *topos* of fragrance in Revelation comes when the author of 1 Enoch links the fragrance of the tree to the healing and wholeness of those in the eschaton. . . . Long life and the lack of 'torment,' 'plague,' and 'suffering' are all consistent with the idea of 'healing' in Revelation 22:2. In light of 1 Enoch 24–25, 4 Ezra 2, and 2 Baruch 29, it is quite likely that the leaves that "heal the nations" in Revelation 22:2 . . . would be heard as fragrant leaves connected to traditions about the fragrant nature of the tree of life."

earth. In other words the great downcoming takes this form: God "will dwell with them; they will be his *peoples* . . ." (Rev. 21:3).[32] That insistent plural may seem barely audible amidst the deafening exceptionalism of "we *the* people." Or of the one and only people of God all along. Besides, it has never been difficult to read the text according to the letter of its exclusions (of those condemned to the "second death") and against the spirit of its celebratory multiplicity. Nevertheless: the divine indwelling can take place only, it appears, within a therapeutic earth-commons. Permeated by the scent of medicine leaves.

And by a mysterious luminosity: "the city has no need of sun or moon to shine on it, for the glory of God is its light, and its lamp is the Lamb." Again one might suppose that the natural creation, or at least the solar system, has been extinguished. But if we dreamread this luminosity theologically rather than astronomically, the "glory" does not appear as overpowering white light but as Lamb-lamp—presumably not a lambskin lampshade but rather a divinanimal immanence.[33] Also a lamp shines only within darkness. The dark becomes luminous: like the "brilliant darkness" of an ancient mysticism, turned on by the spiritual downcoming.[34]

---

32. Revelation here cites the prophet Ezekiel, Ezek. 37:27.

33. For Mayra Rivera, "glory" is a "relational transcendence" that enfolds all. See Mayra Rivera, *Touch of Transcendence: A Postcolonial Theology of God* (Louisville, KY: Westminster John Knox Press, 2007), 129–30. On the theological oscillation between divinity and animality, see the volume that resulted from the eleventh Transdisciplinary Theological Colloquium at Drew University: Stephen D. Moore, ed., *Divinanimality: Animal Theory, Creaturely Theology* (New York: Fordham University Press, 2014).

34. The metaphor of the "brilliant darkness" comes from the fourth-century Gregory of Nyssa, which is developed two centuries later as "negative theology" by Dionysius the Areopagite. For discussion of this heritage, see Catherine Keller, "Enfolding and Unfolding God: Cusanic

The next verse reveals the political hope in play: "the nations will walk by its light, and the kings of the earth will bring their glory into it." We have reflected on how that glory often and tragically turned gory, mistaken for a divinely unified imperium. Yet in the ancient vision-burst, it streams in solidarity with a multiplicity freed from the unitary clutch of Babylon/Rome. The many peoples and kings suggest a pluralism at once ethnic and political, moving with the dignity of their differences through the ever-open gates. So in times of menacing neonationalism, let us vocally mind—as Quakers hold a crisis "in the light"—the implied racial and cultural plurality of the New Jerusalem.

Religiously speaking, something extraordinary takes place here: "I saw no temple in the city, for its temple is the Lord God . . . ." No temple—no cultic sites, no religious institutions, no churches: for God *has become* the temple. As Moltmann puts it, "this city has no temple, because the glory of God is the light and enlightens all inhabitants."[35] This "garden city," the "city of God's kingdom without religion," is the "eschatological city"—not at the end of time but at its coming, its becoming *eschaton,* its "edge." Consequently it is the earthly in-dwelling of the divine that lets the multiplicity live, manifest not in competing "religions" but cooperating peoples. Not in supernatural transcendence but in super, natural immanence.[36]

Down to earth: this is not the come-down of disappointment or of con-descension. Might the erotic metaforce of the bride, in the

---

Complicatio," chap. 3 in *Cloud of the Impossible: Negative Theology and Planetary Entanglement* (New York: Columbia University Press, 2015).

35. Jürgen Moltmann, *Theology of Hope* (New York: Harper & Row, 1967), 84.

36. For naming the shift from the supernatural to the genuinely natural, thanks to ecotheologian Sallie McFague, *Super, Natural Christians: How We Should Love Nature* (Minneapolis: Augsburg Fortress, 1997).

unbridled festivity of this ceremonial downcoming, still lure us to come *down to earth* ourselves? We have never lived elsewhere, anyway. Perhaps a down-to-earth regenesis of our life together is what the new heaven and earth was always about. Or does such improbable *shalom, salaam, salim*[37]—reveal itself as all too utopian? Here where it seems that multinational peace invests in a global market of cutthroat competition, where nationalism claims for the local, where the nations collude not in collective healing but environ*mental* illness —nowhere land is not trending toward good place. But then again, in the eschatological glow of the nonviolent Lamb, the good that is improbable edges away from the merely impossible.

Could we, some critical mass of the species that has trashed the earth, yet recognize it as "cosmic sanctuary"?[38] In an end reflecting and not reiterating the beginning? If we sniff the medicine leaves?

6. Architecture of the Impossible

Back in John's vision: as the New Jerusalem comes down to earth, it lifts cosmopolitanism to bizarrely cosmic heights. And it comes surrounded by a wall. Since John's less visionary commentary can foster supreme exclusions, do we hear—like a farcical echo of its future—"build a wall and make them pay"? Does recent memory still download not a wedding processional but a migrant "caravan" of desperate victims of poverty, racism, climate change seeking— sanctuary? Does it in turn trigger the exodus memory of escaped slaves walking in desperate resolve toward a promised land? And

---

37. "Salim," which is "life" in Korean, seems to share not just the three consonants but an ancient etymological root system with *shalom, salaam*. See Jea Sophia Oh, *A Postcolonial Theology of Life: Planetarity East and West* (Upland, CA: Sopher Press, 2011).

38. "The end mirrors the beginning, recalling Genesis 1's view of creation as God's cosmic sanctuary" (Brown, *Sacred Sense*, 147).

of the biblical imperative: "You must love the immigrants, for you were immigrants in Egypt" (Deut. 10:19). In a time of rising walls—economical, racial, and political—the specifications of the apocalyptic cosmopolis come down in stark rebuff: "Its gates will never be shut by day; and there will be no night there" (Rev. 21:25). In other words these gates are *never closed.*

Why a wall at all? Premodern cities were almost always surrounded by a protective wall. But John imagines a wall unlike any other. Not only structured by twelve gates each made of a giant pearl (no, you won't find Peter guarding these original "pearly gates"), three on each side—encoding at once ethno-political multiplicity (twelve tribes) and cosmic rhythm (twelve months). "The wall is built of jasper." Recall that the "one on the throne" in the opening vision looked not like a human but "like jasper and beryl." So the wall displays a divine minerality. Then comes the colorful gemology of the wall's "foundations," listing twelve precious stones, while the city itself is "clear as glass." The elemental form of divine immanence is here depicted as a many-hued translucency. Its multicolored diversity reflects the multiplicity of the peoples it welcomes.

In this picture of sparkling invitation, the gems dreamread as elemental forms of possibility. No-place actual, they make the good-place possible. Across so many, too many epochs, each gem radiates an enduring brilliance. It almost flashes a picture of what Whitehead called the "primordial nature of God," that aspect of the divine made of pure possibilities—like colors, musical notes, geometries, or complex ideals—that may or may not get actualized in the creative process of the universe.[39] These gem/possibles

---

39. The "pure possibilities" in the primordial divine vision depend upon creaturely collaboration for their actualization. See Alfred North Whitehead, *Process and Reality* (New York: Free Press, 1978), 341–51. For accessible introductions to Whitehead and the process theology he

have the bloodless beauty of abstract forms. We living creatures may ignore them or realize them; we may actualize them a little or a lot, one way or another.

The double-gem deity, in other words, will not, cannot, do our work for us. But it invites us to its place. "I dwell in possibility. . . ."[40] There then can be a warmth of collective comfort, a fragrance of healing—the *apokalypsis* of the new into what in its cool sparkle remains mere utopia, abstract ideal. Its possibility has tantalized us with the chance of an actually civil *civis*, an ecociv to come. Never to be realized perfectly. And as the climate heats up, ever less likely to come at all.

John's architecture within the wall, however, remains measurably bizarre. The text insists on this impossible scale: "The city was foursquare, its length the same as its width . . . fifteen hundred miles, its length and width and height are equal" (Rev. 21:16). That third dimension—*1,500 miles straight up*—makes the New Jerusalem into a monster cube. What's up with this height reaching fifty times farther than earth's atmosphere? What comes down, must rise up? Even as dream-cosmopolis the cubicity daunts. You might almost wonder if John roughly imagined the upward thrusting cities two thousand years in his future, New York, Tokyo, immense boxy structures glittering glassy by day and electrified by night.

More likely, he was transferring the cubic shape of old Jerusalem's holy of holies, at the heart of the (destroyed) temple, onto his city without temples. So the inner sanctum of his people is pro-

---

inspired, see John B. Cobb Jr. and David Ray Griffin, *Process Theology: An Introductory Exposition* (Louisville, KY: Westminster John Knox Press, 1976); Catherine Keller, *On the Mystery: Discerning Divinity in Process* (Minneapolis: Fortress Press, 2008).

40. Emily Dickinson, "I Dwell in Possibility—(466)," in *The Poems of Emily Dickinson: Reading Edition*, ed. Ralph W. Franklin (Cambridge, MA: Belknap Press of Harvard University Press, 1998).

jected as the terrestrial sanctuary of all peoples. At any rate I had tossed the cube into the bin of irrelevance. Then I realized something was tugging at me, something in the very book that had originally lured me into further theological study, John Cobb's *Christ in a Pluralistic Age*.

Its chapter on "The City of God" discusses the visionary architecture of Paolo Soleri. "Until now, cities have been two-dimensional, hence they have overreached themselves and become cancerous. . . . The million small cubes . . . of our homes, buildings etc. . . . could also be formed into *a single large one, with three dimensions*." Soleri's plans take the city *upwards*, within a collective space where people can get everywhere by foot or escalator. Soleri's cities—"arcologies"—are blueprints for sustainability in relation to earth and atmosphere, with social egalitarianism among humans built in. The vast space that is saved by eliminating automobiles, roads, and parking places encourages social vibrancy within the city. At the same time the city opens directly into the surrounding agriculture and wilderness. Of course no arcology, indeed "no city is laid out in a perfect square, and Soleri does not envision building huge solid cubes. After all, he is an artist and a humanist" (and a student of Frank Lloyd Wright). "Throughout his arcology, vast areas are left open for light and air to penetrate. But even if most of the space is left open, the three-dimensional city will occupy barely 1 percent of the land surface of the present two-dimensional city." [41]

None of Soleri's cities have been built. I had visited Arcosanti, where a learning center in the base of a (possible) arcology sits in the Arizona desert. My return visit thirty years later had the feeling of the future-past. Another crumbling might-have-been. Yet the learning center persists.

---

41. John B. Cobb Jr., *Christ in a Pluralistic Age* (Philadelphia: Westminster Press, 1975), 76–77.

Do the gempossibles dissolve into the desert dust of lost chances? Or do they still hint at an architecture of *last* chances?

7. Apocalyptic Conviviality

The trauma of the text of Revelation, not unlike that of human history, never quite resolves. The shadows of human degradation remain. Even though the weaponized word had already taken out all potential enemies of the New Jerusalem, even though its gates stay open 24–7, John assigns himself the role of gatekeeper. "Sorcerers and fornicators and murders and idolaters, and everyone who loves and practices falsehood" —are kept outside (Rev. 22:11). But they are still around. They evidence the utopia's nonsupernatural, earthly status. Yet the aggressive moralism forever stains the text. No doubt he or a later editor was trying to scare contemporaries into exemplary behavior. He warns "anyone who takes away from the words of the book of this prophecy, God will take away that person's share in the tree of life and the city." John thereby marks his voice as second-order commentary upon a closed book. But does his voice of threat not itself "take away from the words" of his own prophecy?

We have dreamread his vision sometimes against himself, trying to surface the trauma-tinged schizopocalypse as a problem for us all. Not that we then hope in text or in time for a utopia of pure inclusion. The text's riffs of resentment belong more to the problem of our civilization than to its solution. They barbwire the open gates. So even at the entrance to the New Jerusalem we cannot mistake Apocalypse for Gospel. John's good city is not the same as Jesus's "good news"—not word of a care that operates no matter what, where, or when.

I do not, however, mean to "take away from the words" of John's needful disclosures. Revelation's no-place does open the possibility of a good place and opens it again and again after it is slammed shut. The dreamy first-order vision comes close to "good news"— it makes *place* for it. It imagines a systemic structure of joyful justice, an architecture of cosmic care. And no armed angelic squads police the wall. Reading John generously, we might rephrase his last-ditch exclusions like this: any down-to-earth human collective will still be haunted by its all-too-human history. It will not simply forget ancient habits of greed and exploitation, even if it largely outgrows them. It does not erase the unoriginal repetitiousness of "original sin." It *minds* it.

New creation is not dissociation. The New Jerusalem remains a vision place of utopian possibility—to be *realized* as best as possible. Not to be left to dry and die as mere ideal.

> here I will give you thunder
> shatter your hearts with rain
> let snow soothe you
> make your healing water
> clear sweet
> a sacred spring
> where the thirsty
> may drink
> animals all
> —bell hooks, "Appalachian Elegy"[42]

And right "through the middle of the street of the city" comes rushing "the river of the water of life, bright as crystal" (Rev. 22:1). Its metaforce sparkles with illimitable grace. With the plurisingular tree of life growing on "both sides" of this river, its cur-

---

42. bell hooks, "Appalachian Elegy (Selections 1–6)," in *Appalachian Elegy* (Lexington: University of Kentucky Press, 2012).

rents recirculate the deep past of Eden's four rivers. Already we heard the earth-bound Alpha-Omega say: "to the thirsty I will give water as a gift from the spring of the water of life" (Rev. 21:6). Insistently Jesus, Spirit, Bride now repeat—"let everyone who is thirsty come" (Rev. 22:17).

Waters of spiritual rehydration, of rebirth, refreshment. And at the same time the sacred spring flows in material restoration: it answers in dream logic the toxification of the earth's waters announced back at the breaking of the seventh seal. There is no separating the physical from the symbolic water of life.[43] In the ancient Near East drought and thirst were frequent threats; water wars loom now. Aquifers all over run low. Potable water is ever bigger business, precisely not to be given as a gift but sold in toxic plastic, further poisoning the "life of the seas."

On this point John could not be more insistent: the water of life is not for sale. "Let anyone who wishes take the water of life as a gift" (Rev. 22:17b). In other words: "The counter-economy of the Apocalypse replaces conspicuous accumulation with conspicuous generosity." Its gift of water allows a cross-cultural comparison with what First Nations call "the Giveaway." And the analogy reveals the other elemental form: "the Sundance, central to Lakoda and Nakoda peoples, also known as the Medicine or Thirst Dance, connects the Giveaway with a sacred dance around

---

43. Jim Perkinson argues that it is "not enough, today, merely to engage the *political* battle over water rights, however; indigenous wisdom and biblical prophecy alike insist that recovery of water *spirituality* is central to a sustainable future." Perkinson animates a "biblical reading for an age of water apocalypse." He draws on indigenous wisdom and biblical prophecy to insist on "the spiritual and political potency of mountains and trees, water and weather, soil and sun and seed." James W. Perkinson, *Political Spirituality for a Century of Water Wars: The Angel of the Jordan Meets the Trickster of Detroit* (New York: Palgrave Macmillan, 2019), 13.

a specially erected tree symbolizing the interconnection of heaven and Earth and the sacred character of all life."[44]

The tree, the water: despite genocidal and ecocidal disregard of life—does the generosity still flow, the connectivity still branch? John's own unhealed trauma might benefit from the indigenous peoples' Medicine Dance. The colonial power of his nightmare beasts is the Roman ancestor of the *Christian* colonial forces that would descend on the First Nations. Waves of subjugation, extermination, commodification—otherwise known as "civilization"—haven't stopped coming. How can the giveaway waters keep coming?

The gift of a water that revives life—*earthly* life—bursts in this last chapter of the Apocalypse into a climactic song of many comings. First comes the fulfillment of the promise of "the Alpha and the Omega, the first and the last," the one who announces: "See, I am coming soon!" (Rev. 22:7). In Christian memory this "I" flows into the voice channeled by the other John: "but those who drink of the water I will give them will never thirst" (John 4:13). Symbolic, material, the giveaway never ceases.

So the "Spirit and the bride say, 'Come.'" The invitation is offered to all who thirst, and simultaneously to their own third,

---

44. "The Giveaway describes a ritual practiced by several Plains First Nations in which wealth or objects of value are ritually given away in order to acknowledge dependence on others for success. Through Giveaway, wealthier members . . . publicly affirm social obligations in using their wealth to promote an equitable distribution of goods." So with no influence here from biblical traditions, the tree of life and the water of life appear together, manifesting the sacrality of interdependent life—in the nonurban utopia of a ritual dance. Harry O. Maier, "There's a New World Coming! Reading the Apocalypse in the Shadow of the Canadian Rockies," in *The Earth Story in the New Testament*, ed. Norman C. Habel and Vicky Balabanski (London: Sheffield Academic Press, 2002), 179.

the Lamb. The coming-down-to-earth of the messianic "I am" was as John wrote still passionately awaited. In some sense he had come already. Although no "Second Coming" is ever mentioned, the messiah remains for John, as for Judaism, the one who is coming—still. "Coming soon" (Rev. 22:7). Soon? Was John just wrong? Hard to dispute. Or may we read "soon" from the perspective of the *eschaton*, the edge of time: which might limn any "now"?[45]

"And let everyone who hears say, 'Come.'" It is as though *we* must yet call God, Messiah, the new cosmopolis *down to earth*. Their triune "coming" requires *our* calling them down. In other words, their immanence needs our invitation. Not metaphysically—if what we name divine signifies an infinity, a boundlessness, it is always already everywhere anyway. But apparently this theotopia needs our invitation in order to *matter*, to materialize, among us. We can no longer separate the life that "comes" from our becoming lives. This new creation won't happen without our desire, our collusion, our creativity. Its renewed and renewing waters and woods, its actually habitable habitats, wild, rural, urban, star-sparkled, depend upon our collective calling. Up to us to *get down* together, to get down to earth with that whole ancient bridal party.

The text now performs a rarely noticed inversion: "And let everyone who is thirsty come." From the inviting down of the one who is "coming soon" *by* "everyone who hears"—it now twists into the inviting *of* "everyone," of all who are in need. Those who thirst—in whichever way—are those who recognize, who *face* their need. At this edge of the scroll a radical relationality tries to reveal itself: the inviters are invited, the callers called. It is as though the messianic always yet "to come" translates into collective becoming. As we learn to dwell mindfully in the "integral

45. Koester, *Revelation*, 839.

ecology" of city, tree, river.[46] To make ourselves at home with the divinity on the ground.

In the mutual immanence of tangled roots, in charred earth and rocky memory, there will still rise big blocks and blockades of hostility. And in answer arises a song of boundless hospitality. Where pestilences separate, we can connect. Where *sur*vival seems uncertain, let *con*viviality—the festivity of life together— break out. The story of gory glory is not over, but its allure is bleeding out. In its place, here in the lamblit dark, what can we—thirsty "animals all"—taste and see? With the *apokalypsis* of opened eyes and "the fragrance of hope," may we discern not a victory march but a medicine dance round the planet?

With it whirls the same old sun, wrapped around the woman in our wilderness. The double-edged tongue licks the wounds it inflicted. The healing tree multiplies across cities, rivers, lakes, oceans. Its perfume drives us wild. Breathe it in deep. Deeper.

---

46. Pope Francis, *Laudato Si': On Care for Our Common Home.*

PostScroll

Any honest apocalypse faces the future. It does not close it down—it pries it open. But what is thereby disclosed? I have been at pains to insist, with old John and without him, that the future does not already exist; it cannot therefore be faced as though it were a fact. That's what "future" means: a present that is not yet. And might never happen. The futures that already exist do so only as possibility. And that means myriad possibilities, a multiverse of possible worlds. We do not read the future.

We read present patterns: how—for instance the stats of global warming—do they trend? We read past patterns—how they worked, how they work still. And with the help of an archaic prophecy, we have dreamread the revealing pattern of an archaic future. That pattern refuses to confine itself to any ancient past, to any abiding present, to any knowable future. So its revelation spirals like a scroll through time. It will not bring us full circle back to some old beginning. It twists (full spiral) through the tense tenses of our own here-and-now. Through the trends, the histories, the dreams.

This meditation has attempted to roll with that scrolling. It might now be summed up something like this—in a sentence (since the Time that Remains is limited): clouds of dark uncertainty keep rolling in, bearing a double-edged disclosure of both the planetary destructiveness of our civilization and the chance—if together we grieve, struggle, and rage out creatively for justice, for transformation social, economic, and ecological—of a festive renewal of our common earth-life.

Perhaps after all I should paraphrase that sentence in terms of the seven strange signs we have probed in these seven chapters. The clouds unfolded in chapter 1, carrying a figure with two-edged tongue, breasts, wooly hair, who turned into Lamb: so we now suffer from cloudy uncertainty about the future of our world, darkly glowing with both dread and possibility. The mourning eagle of chapter 2 calls up our grief at all that is getting needlessly destroyed, human and nonhuman. We are carried by the Sun-woman through horribly difficult births; we are aided by Earth and nourished by her wilderness (chap. 3). As grief grows into rage for justice, for justice social, political, economic, and ecological, the demand for great change risks great violence (chaps. 4, 5, 6). The struggle brings down to earth the Spirit that is always already here: and possibly—just possibly—something somehow like the verdant, loving city once called New Jerusalem opens the gates of our locked-down hope. Even now.

We have dreamread the text away from any recourse to divine control of earth's destiny. Control is not the issue. The issue is what we do, how we live, together. And somehow, sometimes, the Spirit dwells divinely in our togetherness—making it possible. But not making it happen. That is up to us. Us. In whatever collectives and communications, institutions and movements we collect ourselves, we must, we can foster the solidarity that may get us through. Through present crisis to a better here-and-now for all of us earthlings.

That good place in its better time remains almost impossibly possible even now. And that means continuing to hear the eagle's lament. It means rolling with the clouds of dire uncertainty, it means bearing the double-edge of grief turning to anger turning to action—and of action turning to a creativity that weaves us into a world worthy of our best efforts.

And particular actions may fail as they so often have. But they won't have been worthless. Not if we keep faith. With the Spirit of justice, mercy, yes even love. Then your life is caught up in the beauty of a bigger life, a life of all in all. No matter what. And you will feel this when it most matters. You will know that even amidst horrific waste, your efforts, our brief transient realizations, are not wasted—they work together in ways we cannot anticipate for other possible futures. Some much better than others. Some remain off the radar of human understanding.

As for those futures we might understand—or at least dream-read—these trends, histories, and dreams allow us to narrow an infinity of possibilities into a few likely configurations. The possibilities clump like clouds into these most probable human futures. "Probable" because they have already begun. "Human" because we cannot escape a human perspective. We can only change it. As for the "future," it exists only within a present perspective. So as we now scroll down through a set of likely futures, they do not reveal any predictable plan. Any future that pretends to be preset is nothing but a ploy of very present human power.

There appear here seven (what a coincidence) of these cloud-futures. Each expresses a version of anthropocene apocalypse. Each, that is, unveils a future cracking open through unfathomable waste and traumatic destruction. And each retains some relation to the utopian New Jerusalem. But I will not gussy them up with her gowns. These scenes will separate hope from hype.

They begin in the crass opposite of hope.

1. Exhumanity

All too casually now imagined, this future: the extinction of our species. We didn't believe we were just another species, we with our exceptional talents, our godly promise. How could this happen? Seems that it can, and in a now foreseeable future—precisely because of our exceptionalism. This won't be a dignified species death by old age, in hundreds of thousands of years. Nor by unavoidable natural cause, like the collision with the meteor in the film *Melancholia*. We can just stay on course toward climate catastrophe. All this takes is business as usual, though some nuclear outburst would move matters along. Economics, violence, plagues, ecology: name your own four horsepeople. Living by avoidable destruction we die of it. Noble rebellions against extinction fail. No rebooting of *homo sapiens*. Exhumanity.

In face of The End *tout court*, we can only trumpet the closure of Apocalypse. Fine for the fundamentalist version, not for the disclosive original. No one remains to exhume our civilization and learn the lessons we exhumans failed to teach each other. The surviving species that will be better off without us, not to mention species on other planets—may they all thrive. Not our business. Off our radar. Perhaps a residue of us abides in cosmic memory.

A few gems of the unbuilt New Jerusalem still sparkle in the desert sand. RIP, humans.

2. Brute Remainders

Even with the galloping anthropogenic devastations, there could survive pockets of humans. In this scenario, we elude extinction. Some of us remain to grieve and try to rebuild. But instead, brutal marauding and brute survival prevail. *Homo redux*, or descendants we should refrain from naming. No remnants of poetry, scripture, art, technology remain to recycle. Perhaps they wander through some architectural ruins carrying just enough residue of our ten-thousand-year heyday to impart a memorial affect of uncomprehending curiosity and vague resentment.

This neobarbarism cannot be described as Neopaleolithic. The Paleolithic, Neolithic and later tribal humans were living into the challenges of a habitat they had not ruined. Not so for the brute remainder. Better, perhaps, than mere exhumanity. And enough humans may persist for enough centuries that a creative evolution could happen. But such a possibility gives us no excuse for hope. It does not represent a wise new start after great catastrophe, in the biblical sense of Apocalypse or the sci-fi sense of postapocalypse.

Indeed this is true postapocalypse: the memory of the possibility of any New Jerusalem erased.

3. New Jeru for the Few

The global superrich claim the remaining habitable bits of the planet to build estates for themselves. This has already begun. As climate change advances, they expand in this scenario to larger controlled environments for their kind, possibly atmospherically regulated globes, with private armies to guard them and virtual slaves to till the still-arable land they commandeer. Revolts are doomed by high-tech weaponry. Most of the planet's population doesn't need to be killed; they can be let to die of drought, hunger, floods, and desperation. The electronic gates remain closed to them. Day and night. So much for so few. Those will have our long habits of class and race to fortify their walled resolve. They may ironically nickname one of their glittering spheres New Jerusalem. There may unfold centuries of inhumanism, sophisticated in its capacity to absolve itself of its brutality. It would always be the others out there—the ones walled out or the ones "we" might have become—who count as the brutes.

If the memory of a humane possibility festers dis/closively sometime, God bless it.

4. Cybertopia

In this closely related scenario, a greater proportion of humanity may be sustained, inasmuch as they support "progress." They would be integrated into the higher tech civilization toward which we have long been lurching, Orwellian warnings notwithstanding. The mindboggling advance of artificial intelligence will achieve its "posthuman" destination by any means necessary. It can draw along a majority of Northern populations and the elites of the Global South quite voluntarily. We had already become wired to our ubiquitous screens before a pandemic zoomed us along to a qualitative new level of cyberdependence—with its indubitable gifts of low-energy communication at a distance. We might have blocked out the warnings as, well, apocalyptic doom: "The main products of the twenty-first century will be bodies, brains, and minds, and the gap between those who know how to engineer bodies and brains and those who do not . . . will be bigger than the gap between Sapiens and Neanderthals. In the twenty-first century, those who ride the train of progress will acquire divine abilities of creation and destruction, while those left behind will face extinction."[1] The *imago dei* of Genesis has become this *homo deus* of Progress. Its Cyber-Jerusalem can expand indefinitely, its glittering fiber-optics projecting the new heavens and earth into extraterrestrial colonization.

Pause

Each of those four scenarios moves—in wildly diverging ways—with the great extinction spasm that has already begun. Which is the worst? 1, because any human future is done for? 2, because its human(ish) life will barely be worth living in any time frame we can honestly imagine? Or 3 and 4, because the modes of survival are so genocidal and techno-fixed that the earth would be better off without us?

I know only that these options are to be neither ruled out nor expected. If we—you—find us facing such a time, this is still no

---

1. Yuval Noah Harari, *Homo Deus: a Brief History of Tomorrow* (New York: Harper, 2018), 271.

reason to melt into meaninglessness. You still will not know with any certainty which future is realizing itself. At such a point practices of close communal sharing, of neighbor love, of Zen non-clinging, of mystical darkness, of yogic breathing, of ascetic and of aesthetic simplicity, of grieving and of dying well, will be particularly valuable. These practices express an impersonal mindfulness for facing any apocalypse. And they can sustain you there where any collective hope dissolves into illusion. Some intimate communities of survival may take on the indigenous sense of "survivance"—of a vividness, a fullness of life beyond mere survival.[2] New traditions of resistance to brutality and extinction will take root. No matter what.

And even if a viable collective future still has a chance—as in the following three cloud-clumps—apocalyptic mindfulness tracks a double-edge of doom and promise. It tunes to the eagle's cry, the grieving *ouai, ouai.* And so, in the following scenarios, *homo sapiens* actually performs some of its sapientia, not just its smarts. Somehow, as a species—we wise up. We actually morph into a difficult but persistent "we" of multiple peoples and multiple species: we, the earthlings. Any of the following may constellate suddenly, where one of the prior four glooms had been falling. And could collapse again.

5. Village Earth

In this scenario, civilization collapses from ecological catastrophe laced with political terror, pandemic breakdown, and backfiring

---

2. Anishinaabe scholar Gerald Vizenor defines survivance as "an active sense of presence, the continuance of native stories, not a mere reaction, or a survivable name. Native survivance stories are renunciations of dominance, tragedy, and victimry." Gerald Vizenor, *Manifest Manners: Narratives on Postindian Survivance* (Lincoln: University of Nebraska Press, 1999), vii.

technofixes. A neo-Neolithic civilization could emerge from planetary emergency without much surviving civis, but with some sustaining civility. This will take the form primarily of small-scale agricultural communities rather than cities. Even if it can, it will not go urban for its foreseeable future, remembering and relaying how civilization captured, subjugated, and wasted the land, its peoples and its indigenous sapientia. The population collapse that enables this scenario would probably be Armageddonesque and therefore teach grievous lessons. Collective mourning will help to grow mindfully entangled, rooted communities. Those that had already practiced sustainable agriculture will take the lead.

This world of eco-villages seems the opposite of Cybertopia. But network-strengthening virtual communication might not only boost survival and prevent the hardening of boundaries between communities. Wisely dosed, it can circulate a few gems of cosmopolitan diversity, of education and integral ecology. Without some vestige of urban complexity, potential ecovillages could quickly fall into the habits of current white populism, collapsing after all toward the Brute Remains. Spiritual traditions of stranger-love can reroot amidst the ruins of urban civilization as a matter not only of necessity but of conviviality. The collective priority of gardening in the new wilderness—a demanding activity, no return to the original Garden—enfolds our species, like that endangered Sunwoman, in the rigorous care of Earth.

6. Cosmocalypse

Billions die, and die badly. They will also feel for a time like survivors of the end of the world. But unlike Village Earth, a critical mass survives. It requires urban concentrations as well as rural redistributions. Much that civilization has built and learned is recollected, teaching how it betrayed its own better angels. Such angels (not lacking, as we have seen, in militancy) are then mobilized for the new creation, moving us through mourning into revolution against ever-resilient structures—brute, elite, fascist, virtual—of oppression. This would be of these seven the most literal fulfilment of the prophecy of Revelation: upon tragic levels of human and natural cataclysm there finally follows an awesome new city, civis, civilization. Civilization as we haven't known it. Yet it recollects ancestral tribes and nations, inviting their representatives into an immense new architecture of sustainable, sustaining justice. It welcomes them with open gates: dis/closure not closure.

This is apocalypse true to ancient form. In our big ending is our beginning. The new creation is catalyzed by catastrophe. Neither does its New Jerusalem (no virgin for ages) offer a utopia of all-inclusive, static bliss. But its down-to-earth assemblage does produce the new pattern of an ecocivilization. Through continuing challenges of climate and betrayal, it keeps hope in play, on the ground, in a difficult and collaborative earth-commons. It honors—indeed it needs—great difference, human and otherwise: for this is a cosmopolitanism wrapped in cosmos. Against the darkness of space, its starry gown sparkles.

7. The Age of Enlivenment

The seventh scenario shares much with the Cosmocalypse. But it suffers far less mass destruction in the transition. Civilization does not so much explode as twist into ecocivilization: a cosmopolitan legacy survives, almost recognizably, by transformation. We scrape by, ecosocially, in a kind of cloudy historical dialectic that vibrates within great waves of disorder and avoids the worst, but not without grotesque costs. Unregulated capitalism is dethroned through social insistence and ecological sanity; through greener, newer deals we keep the warming to 2(ish) degrees. Haunted by the failed white man enlightenments, we hold to an earth-toned enlivenment. With a modicum of social democracy (by whatever name) we get almost enough trees planted, the population curve curbed, nuclear war avoided, white supremacy broken.[3] The web helps to evolve the reciprocities of local with global, urban with rural. We stumble along in the approximate direction of ecociv.

As with the Cosmocalypse—or any mindful apocalypse—it is the radicality of shared crisis that tears open a depth of new and ancient solidarity. But in this scenario, an enlivenment that we sense even now awakens in enough of us soon enough that we avoid the six above versions of worse. Like a contagion of resurrection, there spreads a spirit of planetarity. Recognized by some as holy, by others as inspiration, it resists the old violence of civilizational hierarchy but revels in the complexities of difference. Between and beyond any religion, calling all species, the immanent spirit does not cease to renew its earth and atmosphere. New creation not *ex nihilo* but *ex profundis*—in a chaos now minded for its eye-opening apocalypses. I suspect most of us who are not denialists or nihilists press toward this modest and mixed, graciously down-to-earth outcome. And in imagining its chance we enliven our actuality.

The point is, of course, that each of these scenarios is implicated in the others and in its own unknowability. Even the worst, mere extinction, can only be faced by one who is not yet extinguished. And if there is one, that one cannot know that there aren't enough others that something, somehow, else is possible. Some fragrant, festive co-habitation of earthlings.

---

3. Gary Dorrien, *Breaking White Supremacy: Martin Luther King Jr. and the Black Social Gospel* (New Haven: Yale University Press, 2020).

"The Garden of Impending Bloom"

Those words were scrawled on a little hand-painted sign I saw last summer. It was tacked on a wire fence surrounding a bit of desolate, apparently toxically compromised land by a parking lot in a small urban area of a western state. A tawdry scene. Its message won't leave me alone. Maybe it will come to you too, sometime when you are facing apparent doom.

The End?

Acknowledgments

No doubt I must first of all thank old John of Patmos for writing his darkly hopeful Apocalypse a couple thousand years ago. Despite the endless texts about his text (and now another) his spirit is not laid to rest. It haunts history. Since we fail to exorcise his ghost, we may exhort its cooperation. May we continue to call upon his better angels—there are some awful ones—to inspire gracious realizations of the vision. World-realizations, beyond any books about the Book of Revelation.

Yet for this book, most of my gratitude goes to a great host of live and enlivening readers.

I got indispensable support from present and former students. O'neil Van Horn passed crucial gems of song and poetry my way. As research assistants, Hunter Bragg offered innumerable revealing insights; Dan Siedell tendered relevant aesthetics; Winfield Goodwin contributed disclosive tidbits. Byron Belitsos, an author tuned to benign celestials, offered on-the-ground publishing wisdom. And without J. D. Mechelke, who carried with rigor and cheer a great burden of editorial and bibliographic labor, who knows when I would have finished the manuscript?

Friends facilitated this writing at every stage. Early on, Deb Ullman and Cynthia Beebe helped me consider nontheological, nonacademic readers. Despite my lack of Sanskrit, Loriliai Biernacki lent early and breath-deepening insights. Marcia Pally, a most relational political theologian, offered a crucial reading of the manuscript. My friend of four decades, feminist literary scholar Mary DeShazer, kicked in when the book most needed her, speedily enhancing the language and lucidity of last drafts.

In a category all his own, Sam Castleberry burst into the force-field of this project. With brilliant insistence he commented upon one version, and then another, and . . . what a gift.

Underneath it all lies the support of the Association of Theological Schools, permitting me—with the encouragement of Dean Javier Viera and Drew's Theological School—the privilege of a Henry Luce III Fellowship in Theology for 2017–2018. Thanks to Stephen Graham and Jonathan van Antwerpen for their crucial theological leadership, and for memorable conversations with fellow Fellows Bill Brown and Emmanuel Katongole, as well as formal respondent John Thatamanil, friend and theologian extraordinaire.

The *sine qua non* of publication is of course the publisher. This book has been enhanced in content and form by the multi-orbed involvement of Robert Ellsberg of Orbis Books. Let me thank also the crucial contributions of Paul Kobelski and of Managing Editor Maria Angelini.

And from Jason, partner through whichever apocalypses come our way, streams a music beyond language.

Index